Same-Sex Marriage

Other Books in the Current Controversies Series

Same-Sex Marriage

Tamara Thompson, Book Editor

GREENHAVEN PRESS
A part of Gale, Cengage Learning

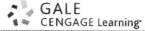

Farmington Hills, Mich • San Francisco • New York • Waterville, Maine
Meriden, Conn • Mason, Ohio • Chicago

Patricia Coryell, *Vice President & Publisher, New Products & GVRL*
Douglas Dentino, *Manager, New Products*
Judy Galens, *Aquisitions Editor*

For more information, contact:
Greenhaven Press
27500 Drake Rd.
Farmington Hills, MI 48331-3535
Or you can visit our Internet site at gale.cengage.com

Articles in Greenhaven Press anthologies are often edited for length to meet page requirements. In addition, original titles of these works are changed to clearly present the main thesis and to explicitly indicate the author's opinion. Every effort is made to ensure that Greenhaven Press accurately reflects the original intent of the authors. Every effort has been made to trace the owners of copyrighted material.

Cover image © Cindy Hughes/Shutterstock.com.

LIBRARY OF CONGRESS CATALOGING-IN-PUBLICATION DATA

Same-sex marriage / Tamara Thompson, book editor.
    pages cm. -- (Current controversies)
    Includes bibliographical references and index.
    ISBN 978-0-7377-7219-7 (hardcover) -- ISBN 978-0-7377-7220-3 (pbk.)
    1. Same-sex marriage--United States. 2. Same-sex marriage. I. Thompson, Tamara.
    HQ1034.U5S24 2015
    306.84'8--dc23
                                                    2014032377

Printed in the United States of America
1 2 3 4 5 6 7 19 18 17 16 15

Contents

Edith Windsor married her partner of forty years in Canada but when her spouse died, Windsor faced huge estate taxes because the US government did not recognize their marriage. Windsor's unequal treatment under the law led the US Supreme Court to overturn the Defense of Marriage Act (DOMA) in June 2013.

Chapter 2: Does Same-Sex Marriage Benefit Society?

Same-sex marriage benefits society because it promotes equality and nondiscrimination, generates economic opportunities, fosters mental and physical well-being, supports family stability, and bolsters the international reputation of the United States, among other positive effects.

Allowing same-sex couples to marry would fundamentally change the meaning of marriage for future generations, further eroding the crucial role the institution plays in strengthening society. Same-sex relationships are also harmful to society because LGBT people engage in more promiscuous behaviors and offer a less stable home environment for raising children, among other serious concerns.

Chapter 3: Is Same-Sex Marriage Good for Families and Children?

No matter how stable and loving a same-sex household is, children deeply feel the absence of a male or female parent. Same-sex parenting is an emotional hardship for children that creates a lasting impact on their psyches.

Chapter 4: What Are Some Other Key Issues with Same-Sex Marriage?

Foreword

By definition, controversies are "discussions of questions in which opposing opinions clash" (*Webster's Twentieth Century Dictionary Unabridged*). Few would deny that controversies are a pervasive part of the human condition and exist on virtually every level of human enterprise. Controversies transpire between individuals and among groups, within nations and between nations. Controversies supply the grist necessary for progress by providing challenges and challengers to the status quo. They also create atmospheres where strife and warfare can flourish. A world without controversies would be a peaceful world; but it also would be, by and large, static and prosaic.

The Series' Purpose

The purpose of the Current Controversies series is to explore many of the social, political, and economic controversies dominating the national and international scenes today. Titles selected for inclusion in the series are highly focused and specific. For example, from the larger category of criminal justice, Current Controversies deals with specific topics such as police brutality, gun control, white collar crime, and others. The debates in Current Controversies also are presented in a useful, timeless fashion. Articles and book excerpts included in each title are selected if they contribute valuable, long-range ideas to the overall debate. And wherever possible, current information is enhanced with historical documents and other relevant materials. Thus, while individual titles are current in focus, every effort is made to ensure that they will not become quickly outdated. Books in the Current Controversies series will remain important resources for librarians, teachers, and students for many years.

In addition to keeping the titles focused and specific, great care is taken in the editorial format of each book in the series. Book introductions and chapter prefaces are offered to provide background material for readers. Chapters are organized around several key questions that are answered with diverse opinions representing all points on the political spectrum. Materials in each chapter include opinions in which authors clearly disagree as well as alternative opinions in which authors may agree on a broader issue but disagree on the possible solutions. In this way, the content of each volume in Current Controversies mirrors the mosaic of opinions encountered in society. Readers will quickly realize that there are many viable answers to these complex issues. By questioning each author's conclusions, students and casual readers can begin to develop the critical thinking skills so important to evaluating opinionated material.

Current Controversies is also ideal for controlled research. Each anthology in the series is composed of primary sources taken from a wide gamut of informational categories including periodicals, newspapers, books, US and foreign government documents, and the publications of private and public organizations. Readers will find factual support for reports, debates, and research papers covering all areas of important issues. In addition, an annotated table of contents, an index, a book and periodical bibliography, and a list of organizations to contact are included in each book to expedite further research.

Perhaps more than ever before in history, people are confronted with diverse and contradictory information. During the Persian Gulf War, for example, the public was not only treated to minute-to-minute coverage of the war, it was also inundated with critiques of the coverage and countless analyses of the factors motivating US involvement. Being able to sort through the plethora of opinions accompanying today's major issues, and to draw one's own conclusions, can be a complicated and frustrating struggle. It is the editors' hope that Current Controversies will help readers with this struggle.

Introduction

> *"Both supporters and opponents of same-sex marriage agree that the normalization of same-sex relationships in mainstream culture has been key to the dramatic shift, though they hold vastly different views about what that means."*

On May 18, 1970, Jack Baker and Michael McConnell walked into the Hennepin County courthouse in Minneapolis and applied for a marriage license, but their application was flatly denied because both University of Minnesota students were men. The couple sued for the right to marry but lost despite taking the case all the way to the US Supreme Court. It would be another forty years before the nation's highest court again considered the issue of same-sex marriage.

Three years after Baker and McConnell tried to become the first legally married gay couple in US history, Maryland became the first state to pass a law specifically banning same-sex marriage. Over the following decades—as the LGBT (lesbian, gay, bisexual, and transgender) movement gained political clout and state courts began upholding marriage rights for same-sex couples—dozens of states instituted similar bans, either by legislative statue or by voter-approved amendments to their state constitutions.

The federal government itself enacted the Defense of Marriage Act (DOMA), legislation signed by President Bill Clinton in 1996 that formally defined marriage as a union between one man and one woman. Under DOMA, the federal government refused to recognize same-sex marriages performed in any state that legalized them (Massachusetts was the first in 2004), and the newly codified definition of marriage affected a wide variety of laws governing eligibility for 1,138 practical, financial, and legal benefits, rights, and responsibilities from the federal government and hundreds more from the states.

One of those rights is inheriting property without taxation when a spouse dies, a routine transfer of assets for widowed heterosexual people. It was anything but routine for Edith Windsor, however, after her lesbian partner of forty years died in 2009. Though the two New York residents had been legally married in Canada, the US government would not recognize their marriage because of DOMA, and Windsor got hit with a huge estate tax bill.

Windsor sued the US government and her case ultimately led to the landmark Supreme Court decision on June 26, 2013, that Section 3 of DOMA, the clause defining marriage, was unconstitutional. Two days later, the federal government extended its employee spousal benefits to legally married same-sex couples regardless of their state of residence.

Other federal agencies updated their affected regulations and programs over the next eight months, including revisions to rules governing income taxes, inheritance, Social Security, immigration, pensions, prison visits, and the ability to refuse to testify against a spouse in federal court. Most of the changes apply to married same-sex couples regardless of where they live, but the requirements of some federal laws on Social Security, family leave, and veterans' benefits have created complications that have yet to be worked out for couples living in states that do not recognize same-sex marriages from other states.

Following DOMA's demise and the federal government's quick enactment of its remedies, several states gave up on defending their same-sex marriage bans and others have since seen their bans overturned by courts. According to Freedom to Marry, a same-sex marriage advocacy group, more than 38 percent of the US population now lives in a state that either permits same-sex marriage or recognizes the out-of-state marriages of same-sex couples.

As of August 2014, nineteen states and the District of Columbia were performing same-sex marriages, nineteen states still had constitutional bans on same-sex marriage in place, and twelve states had their bans overturned by the courts but the rulings have been stayed while they are under appeal.

Those numbers are certain to change in the months and years ahead, however. News headlines reflect daily changes in the status of same-sex marriage in states nationwide and only five state marriage bans are not currently being challenged in state or federal court, according to reporting by the Gay, Lesbian, Bisexual and Transgender News Network.

Aside from the far-reaching legal impact of DOMA's reversal, one of the most remarkable things about the court's decision is that Jack Baker and Michael McConnell, the Minnesota couple from 1970, were around to see it. That a shift of such magnitude and breadth took place during their lifetimes represents perhaps the biggest and most rapid transformation of culture and politics the United States has ever experienced on a single issue.

"It's unusual to see this much change in a relatively short amount of time,"[1] says Robert P. Jones, chief executive officer of the Public Religion Research Institute (PRRI), which released an in-depth study on same-sex marriage in February 2014.

"In the decade since Massachusetts became the first state to legalize same-sex marriage, Americans' support for allowing gay and lesbian people to legally wed has jumped 21 percent-

---

1. Quoted in Cathy Lynn Grossman, "Survey: Americans Turn Sharply Favorable on Gay Issues," *Religion News Service*, February 26, 2014. http://www.religionnews.com/2014/02/26/gay-marriage-lgbt-prri-pew-religion.

age points, from 32 percent in 2003 to 53 percent in 2013,"[2] the PRRI study found. Numerous other opinion polls from 2013 consistently put public support of same-sex marriage at or above that figure, double the 27 percent approval rating that Gallup reported when it first posed the question in 1996.

Both supporters and opponents of same-sex marriage agree that the normalization of same-sex relationships in mainstream culture has been key to the dramatic shift, though they hold vastly different views about what that means.

Back in 1997, when Ellen DeGeneres came out as a lesbian on her TV sitcom, it was a big controversy and advertisers dropped her show. Today, DeGeneres hosts the Oscars and a popular talk show, and gay characters are a regular part of series such as *Grey's Anatomy*, *Glee*, *Modern Family*, and *The New Normal*.

While the LGBT community and same-sex marriage supporters celebrate that as evidence of progress, opponents say it is instead evidence of the problem.

"The movement to normalize homosexual behavior has exploded on the American scene,"[3] states Donald E. Wildmon, founder and chairman emeritus of the American Family Association, a Christian nonprofit organization. "We oppose the efforts of the homosexual movement to force its agenda on our sentiments in schools, government, business and workplaces through law, public policy and media. Our strong opposition is a reaction to the homosexual movement's aggressive strategies."[4]

2. Public Religion Research Institute, "American Religious Landscape Transforming as Support for Same-Sex Marriage Dramatically Increases," February 26, 2014. http://publicreligion.org/newsroom/2014/02/2014-lgbt-survey.

3. Quoted in Jeremy Hooper, "The American Family Association's Agenda in Its Founder's Own Words," GLAAD, October 16, 2013. https://www.glaad.org/blog/american-family-associations-agenda-its-founders-own-words.

4. Ibid.

Indeed, the PRRI study shows that one of the LGBT movement's most longstanding strategies to raise visibility and further mainstream acceptance has proved highly effective in changing hearts and minds on the same-sex marriage issue: "coming out" by publically revealing one's sexual orientation to friends and family members.

As LGBT people came out and became more visible in mainstream communities throughout the 1990s and 2000s, people from all walks of life discovered that they had friends, neighbors, coworkers, and family members who were lesbian or gay.

"Few changes over the last 20 years have had a more profound effect on support for same-sex marriage than the increasing number of people who now have a gay friend or family member,"[5] notes PRRI research director Daniel Cox. That number, he says, "has increased by a factor of three over the last two decades, from 22 percent in 1993 to 65 percent today."

The PRRI survey concluded that Americans who have an LGBT friend or family member are 1.75 times more likely to support legalizing same-sex marriage (63 percent vs. 36 percent), an indication that the marriage-equality movement has evolved from being a fringe issue for most straight people to being seen as a mainstream civil rights issue that affects the lives of people they care about, if not their own.

The authors in *Current Controversies: Same-Sex Marriage* represent a wide range of viewpoints on key questions about the history and status of same-sex marriage in the United States; whether it is beneficial or harmful to society, families, and children; and what the ongoing transformation of the marriage landscape means for traditional marriage, religious freedom, the economy, ongoing LGBT activism, and transgender people.

---

5. Op. cit.

CHAPTER 1

How Did Same-Sex Marriage Become Legal in the United States?

Overview: The Complex Issue of Same-Sex Marriage

David Lampo

David Lampo is director of publications at the Cato Institute, a libertarian think tank based in Washington, DC.

Same-sex marriage has frightened and enraged opponents of gay rights more than any other issue. It's so charged with emotion and symbolism on both sides that we all need to pause, take a deep breath, and analyze the issues involved in a calm and rational manner. Here is a brief review of the events that brought us to where we are today in this debate.

Few people either inside or outside the gay community had ever seriously discussed marriage rights until the 2003 *Goodridge v. Department of Public Health* decision that legalized same-sex marriage in Massachusetts. One of the first, and perhaps the most prominent, exceptions was Andrew Sullivan, a gay conservative who was then editor at the *New Republic*, a liberal opinion magazine based in Washington, DC. In 1989, Sullivan penned a piece titled "Here Comes the Groom: A Conservative Case for Gay Marriage," in which he argued that grafting a conservative social institution such as marriage onto the gay and lesbian communities would help provide the same stability and security it does to heterosexual families. Some in the gay community have vilified Sullivan and other gay advocates of same-sex marriage for selling out the gay community by supporting marriage and thereby reinforcing patriarchy and other alleged evils of capitalist society. Ironically, this issue has created an odd alliance of Far Left and Far Right in their joint opposition to marriage equality.

The first high-profile legal case involving same-sex marriage took place in Hawaii in 1993, when the state's supreme court ruled that Hawaii's law against same-sex marriage was unconstitutional unless there was a compelling state interest in banning it. Before the ruling could take effect, in 1998, Hawaiians voted overwhelmingly to amend the state constitution to give the legislature the power to restrict marriage to opposite-sex couples only. . . .

The Rise of DOMA

The Hawaii case prompted a swift reaction from the federal government. In 1996, Congress overwhelmingly passed the Defense of Marriage Act (DOMA), which formally defined marriage for federal government purposes as a union between one man and one woman. DOMA also denied federal benefits for same-sex couples and relieved states of any legal obligation to recognize same-sex marriages performed in other states. Most Democrats and virtually all Republicans voted for DOMA as it passed the Senate by an 85–14 vote and the House by a 342–67 margin. President Bill Clinton signed the measure into law. The law did not change or affect state laws regarding marriage, and some may have thought (or hoped) that it would end the increasingly contentious issue.

Media coverage of [the] San Francisco marriages was intense, and the national reaction to both them and the Massachusetts court decision was swift and furious.

Things remained quiet on the marriage equality front until 2003, when the national debate on this issue reignited. The spark was a lawsuit in Massachusetts. In the *Goodridge* case, the Massachusetts Supreme Judicial Court declared that state's law against same-sex marriage violated the state constitution. The ruling made Massachusetts only the sixth jurisdiction in the world at the time to permit same-sex marriage, along with the Netherlands, Belgium, Ontario, British Columbia, and Quebec (since then, Argentina, Canada, Iceland, Norway, South Africa, Spain, Sweden, and Portugal have legalized same-sex marriage). In the United States, the District of Columbia and six other states have also instituted same-sex marriage: Connecticut, Iowa, New Hampshire, Vermont, Washington, and New York. In 2009, Maine's legislature adopted gay marriage, but the state's voters overturned that law within months.

Subsequent attempts in Massachusetts to overturn the court's decision failed when the state legislature voted in 2007 against putting a repeal measure on the ballot, effectively giving gay marriage in that state the legislature's seal of approval. Even many original opponents of gay marriage in Massachusetts have changed their minds. Massachusetts now has sixteen thousand gay married couples, and yet, contrary to predictions by opponents of gay marriage, divorce rates in Massachusetts have dropped and are now the lowest in the country.

A San Francisco Backlash

In March 2004, San Francisco city officials began issuing marriage licenses to same-sex couples in violation of California state law. Over three thousand couples married before the California Supreme Court declared the marriages null and void. Media coverage of these San Francisco marriages was intense, and the national reaction to both them and the Massachusetts court decision was swift and furious. In 2004, thirteen states voted to ban gay marriage at the ballot box. The narrowest margin of victory was in Oregon, with 57 percent in favor; in states like Kentucky, Georgia, and Arkansas, the ban passed by more than three to one, and in Mississippi, it passed by six to one. It was not surprising that something as shocking and new to the average American provoked such a strong response. Anti-gay rights organizations such as the Family Research Council, Focus on the Family, and the American Family Association crowed about the wins. And it wasn't just marriage that was banned; some states also banned civil unions and domestic partnerships.

Coming on the heels of the Massachusetts court decision, the San Francisco marriages fueled the calls for the Federal Marriage Amendment, which would have written the definition of "traditional" marriage into the US Constitution and barred states from adopting marriage equality, even if done democratically at the ballot box or legislatively by state lawmakers. Although this proposal became the top national priority of anti-gay rights groups, it failed in two attempts to gain enough Republican votes in the US Senate and effectively died in 2006, even before Democrats took control of the Senate in November of that year, killing any chance that the amendment would be reconsidered. Few Senate Republicans have any interest in refighting a lost battle heading into the 2012 election, although most of the Republican presidential field still supported such a measure, including Mitt Romney, Rick Santorum, Michele Bachmann, Tim Pawlenty, Herman Cain, Newt Gingrich, and Rick Perry.

Any discussion [of same-sex marriage] must begin with the recognition that there is both a civil and a religious component to marriage, and each is very different.

State Bans on Same-Sex Marriage

More gay marriage bans followed the first round in 2004, although with smaller margins of victory. Twenty-nine states now have constitutional bans on gay marriage, while nine others have statutes that outlaw it. Although some of these states, such as California, have strong (almost marriage-like) protections for same-sex couples, most do not, and at least nineteen of the states that prohibit gay marriage also prohibit any legal recognition of gay couples. Three states—New York, Maryland, and Rhode Island—recognize out-of-state gay marriages, but same-sex unions cannot be performed in Maryland or Rhode Island.

The architects of state marriage bans have, for the most part, been socially conservative and Religious Right voters and leaders associated with the Republican Party, although black pastors have helped lead the fight in some states and the District of Columbia. The Massachusetts court decision has proved a financial boon to their organizations, and although opposition to gay marriage has waned considerably over the past few years, Religious Right leaders have been effective at exploiting voters' confusion and anger about same-sex marriage.

There are three important issues to consider in this debate:

1. the merits and justice of same-sex marriage or other forms of relationship recognition;

2. the position of the American people in general and Republicans in particular regarding legal recognition of same-sex couples; and

3. the best process for obtaining same-sex marriage: through the courts, the state legislature, the ballot box, or all three.

The Civil Component of Marriage

Some opponents of same-sex marriage are so emotionally and unalterably opposed to homosexuality and gay unions that it's not really possible to have a rational discussion about the issue. But for everyone else, any discussion must begin with the recognition that there is both a civil and a religious component to marriage, and each is very different.

The marriage license is the civil part of marriage and has nothing to do with religion or church in any legal sense. It is a government license allowing two people to join in the marriage contract. Obtaining the license requires no religious belief, of course, and no intent to produce offspring: it makes no mention of either. To complete the marriage process, two people need only find a justice of the peace or some other legally sanctioned person to conduct the ceremony. The marriage license doesn't even require that both parties love one another. It is, totally and completely, a document that simply binds two people together from a legal perspective, be they Christian, atheist, or anything else. Proponents of marriage equality focus on this aspect of marriage: equal access for same-sex couples to the license and the many benefits that come with it. This includes not just the stability and security of a stable, legally protected relationship but also the monetary benefits and numerous legal protections as well. The US Government Accounting Office lists 1,138 legal rights, monetary benefits, and responsibilities that come with marriage, all now denied to both unmarried straight and same-sex couples, from tax equity (excluding health insurance benefits from taxable income) to spousal Social Security benefits.

The Religious Component of Marriage

The other major aspect of marriage is religious in nature. This is the ceremonial part of marriage that usually takes place in a church or temple, although millions do not participate in this aspect of marriage when they tie the proverbial knot. Marriage, of course, has immense religious significance to people of faith, although its meaning and significance varies greatly from religion to religion and especially from culture to culture. The religious aspect of marriage is clearly secondary from a legal perspective, however, because it is not required in order to execute a marriage; only a marriage license and a justice of the peace are required to do that. A couple can have the most elaborate and meaningful religious ceremony possible, and many do, but that ceremony and the church's blessing are neither necessary nor sufficient to execute a legally recognized marriage. Many religious people have labeled marriage a "holy union" before God, but such a belief or description has no legal standing whatsoever—nor should it.

The marriage license . . . mandates no belief in God, and, certainly, thousands of nonbelievers get married every year, illustrating yet again the nonreligious nature of civil marriage.

The first reaction of most opponents of gay marriage is to raise various religious objections to both homosexuality and same-sex unions. Apart from the important fact that some Christian denominations (such as Episcopalians, the United Church of Christ, Quakers, some Methodists, Unitarians, and others) sanction same-sex unions, these opponents are forgetting that the marriage license is a civil, not a religious, document. It favors no particular religious group or its views on homosexuality. It is not a stamp of approval—only a permission slip, if you will, to get married. Religious arguments against extending it to same-sex couples should be irrelevant in a country that boasts freedom of religion.

Other opponents of same-sex marriage say the primary purpose of marriage is procreation, but that is clearly false for millions of married people. The marriage license contains no requirement whatsoever to produce children, and in fact, no religion makes procreation a requirement for receiving its blessing or participating in its sacraments. Millions of heterosexuals in this country who have no intention of procreating, or who are too old or unable to do so, obtain their marriage licenses, get married, and receive the blessing of their respective churches.

The marriage license also mandates no belief in God, and, certainly, thousands of nonbelievers get married every year, illustrating yet again the nonreligious nature of civil marriage. Perhaps that is why the activists in the ranks of the Religious Right want a theocracy. They realize America is a secular state under which we have no religious requirements to hold office: we have mostly secular citizens as elected leaders—not ministers, priests, rabbis, or mullahs.

"A Continuously Evolving Institution"

Opponents of marriage equality sometimes fall back on the "tradition" argument: marriage, they say, has always been between one man and one woman, and we should therefore not redefine it. But again, that is historically inaccurate. Polygamy was referred to, but not condemned, throughout the Old Testament, and as conservative *New York Times* columnist Ross Douthat has pointed out, "The default family arrangement in many cultures, modern as well as ancient, has been polygamy, not monogamy." Nor is "lifelong heterosexual monogamy obviously natural in the way that most Americans understand the term," he writes. "If 'natural' is defined to mean 'congruent with our biological instincts,' it's arguably one of the more unnatural arrangements imaginable." Perhaps this fact explains the widespread polygamy, adultery, and even harems common in cultures around the world throughout human history, as well as today.

Marriage has, in fact, been a continuously evolving institution. Only in the sixteenth century, for example, did marriage begin to resemble what we have today—that is, one man united to one woman. Even then, marriages were often arranged by the families of the bride and groom, and women traditionally had few, if any, legal rights in the relationship. They were essentially property, first of their fathers and then of their husbands, and they were expected to do what they were told. And they did. Child brides were common, and marriages were more often about social status and political power than the idealized holy matrimony that today's "defenders" of marriage romanticize about.

The argument . . . that modern marriage is primarily a religious sacrament is false: a religious sacrament has no legal basis.

By the time of the Reformation in the sixteenth century, most Protestants saw little reason for church involvement with marriage, which was considered more the purview of the state than the church. Martin Luther himself wrote, "Since marriage has existed from the beginning of the world and is still found among unbelievers, there is no reason why it should be called a sacrament of the New Law and of the church alone." Marriage was becoming primarily an institution of government regarding its legal basis and whatever contractual rights it included.

The rise of classical liberalism, the philosophical ancestor of modern libertarianism, cemented this quite radical change, which, according to evangelical author John Witte, emphasized the contractual and consensual nature of marriage. Exponents of this view, he writes, "advocated the abolition of much that was considered . . . sacred in the Western legal tradition of marriage. They urged the abolition of the requirements of parental consent, church consecration, and formal witnesses for marriage. They questioned the exalted status of heterosexual monogamy, suggesting that such matters be left to private negotiation. They called for the absolute equality of husband and wife to receive, hold, and alienate property, to enter into contracts and commerce, to participate on equal terms in the workplace and in the public square. They castigated the state for leaving annulment practice to the church, and urged that the laws of annulment and divorce be both merged and expanded under exclusive state jurisdiction."

The Legal Foundation of Marriage

The argument, then, that modern marriage is primarily a religious sacrament is false: a religious sacrament has no legal basis. Only the civil aspect of marriage has a legal foundation, which is the marriage license and the legal rights inherent in it.

That legal foundation continues to change. As recently as 1967, for example, interracial marriages in the United States were illegal, often based on the rationale that the scriptures forbade such unions, the same argument we hear today about same-sex unions. Only when the Supreme Court intervened in the case *Loving v. Virginia* were state laws banning such marriages overturned. Would the current opponents of same-sex marriage who rail about judges getting involved in the same-sex marriage debate have damned the Supreme Court's 9–0 decision in this case as "judicial activism"? It's doubtful. In fact, that brilliantly argued decision states that marriage is a "basic civil right. . . . The freedom to marry, or not marry, a person of another race resides with the individual and cannot be infringed by the State." The fundamental justice behind that decision is universal and provides the basis and rationale for legalizing same-sex marriage.

The often heard argument that marriage as we know it is "under attack" because of the effort to legalize same-sex marriage is really inexplicable. It is bizarre to believe that allowing the small fraction of the population that would participate in same-sex marriage to do so would somehow pose a danger to the overwhelmingly heterosexual nature of the institution. How is granting to same-sex couples the same legal rights that come with the marriage license any threat at all to heterosexual marriage? In fact, many argue that spreading the institution of marriage to previously excluded gay couples would only strengthen it and widen its appeal.

Surely, with the high rate of divorce and declining rate of heterosexual marriage in the United States, the institution of marriage could use some help. Clearly, its decline, which has been going on for at least forty years, has had nothing to do with the recent emergence of same-sex marriage.

> *Trying to force-feed certain cultural and religious values to the American public, through legal sanctions and preferences, is both destined to fail and distinctly un-American.*

Addressing the real causes of the breakdown of the heterosexual family would seem a much better target for those who spend their time and money opposing same-sex marriage. Government statistics show that 40 percent of children today are born out of wedlock to heterosexual parents (70 percent among blacks). Yet much of the Religious Right is obsessed with homosexuality and the prospect of same-sex marriage. Wouldn't these opponents be wiser to tend to the systematic breakdown of heterosexual marriage caused by . . . heterosexuals?

The Popularity of Marriage Is Declining

The fact is that the popularity of marriage as an institution has dropped drastically over the past sixty years. According to the US Census Bureau, married-couple households now constitute less than half of the households in the United States. In 1950, married couples made up over 78 percent of American households; today, that number has dropped to 49.7 percent. There are various reasons for this dramatic change, but the fact is that social mores and values are very different than they were sixty years ago. As much as religious fundamentalists might like to, America is not going back to what some might consider "the good old days." Trying to force-feed certain cultural and religious values to the American public, through legal sanctions and preferences, is both destined to fail and distinctly un-American. As social values continue to evolve, traditional Christians really have no choice but to evolve with them. They might not like the inevitable social change that is taking place, but in a free society, their only legitimate response can be to proselytize, not persecute.

Out of desperation, some opponents of marriage equality raise the specter of their churches and ministers being forced to sanction same-sex couples if we legalize same-sex marriage. The prospect of a fundamentalist denomination or the Catholic Church being forced to recognize or perform such marriages must be truly frightening to many people. But the spokesmen who use such imaginary threats to raise money and frighten their parishioners must realize these scary scenarios are completely fictional.

No credible proponent of marriage equality has ever proposed empowering the government to force any religious institution to sanction, recognize, or perform gay marriages (or even to admit gay members). In fact, those states that permit such marriages have specific legal guarantees against such imaginary threats. No church or minister in any state that now has gay marriage can honestly claim otherwise. . . .

Growing Support for Same-Sex Marriage

The trend line of growing support for same-sex marriage has been clear for some time, and no one seriously expects that trend to change.

Polls from 2009 alone demonstrate the evolution in public opinion. An NBC/*Wall Street Journal* poll from October showed 41 percent in favor of same-sex marriage and 49 percent opposed which was then the lowest level of opposition in fourteen years. While a Quinnipiac poll from that same year showed just 38 percent in support with 55 percent opposed, an April 30, 2009, ABC News/*Washington Post* poll showed 49 percent in support with 46 percent opposed. Public opinion was clearly beginning to change, perhaps due in part to all the publicity garnered by the 2008 Proposition 8 vote in California and subsequent court battle.

Not only is support for gay marriage growing across the board, but the intensity of support is also increasing.

That shift began to accelerate in 2010, with a small but consistent majority developing in favor of same-sex marriage according to most major pollsters. An August 2010 Associated Press poll, for example, revealed a 52 percent majority in favor of the government giving legal recognition to marriage between same-sex couples, with 46 percent opposed. This included 25 percent of Republicans.

A March 2011 ABC News/*Washington Post* poll showed a slim majority, 53 percent, in favor of same-sex marriage, with 47 percent opposed, a complete reversal in just two years. While a March 2011 poll from Pew Research Center showed the nation evenly split, 45 percent in favor of same-sex marriage with 46 percent opposed, an April CNN poll showed a 51 to 47 percent majority in favor. And a Gallup poll in May 2011 showed a 53 to 45 percent majority. A consistent pattern of support had clearly emerged, surprising even advocates.

Several polls later in the year demonstrated continuing growth in support for same-sex marriage. An August poll by the Associated Press and the National Constitution Center found that 53 percent of Americans supported marriage equality, a slight increase from the previous year. Another poll by the Public Religion Research Institute (PRRI) showed the country evenly divided at 47 percent each, the first time in the PRRI poll that support for same-sex marriage was not a minority position. It also showed nearly a third (31 percent) of Republicans in support, 49 percent of Republican Millennials (ages eighteen to twenty-nine) in support, and even 44 percent of evangelical Millennials. Finally, a Pew Research Center poll in November revealed a plurality of 46 percent support- ing gay marriage, with 44 percent opposed. This was a switch from just ten months earlier, when a plurality of respondents opposed same-sex marriage. Polling in 2012 will no doubt show that support for same-sex marriage continues to grow.

Growing Intensity

Not only is support for gay marriage growing across the board, but the intensity of support is also increasing; at the same time, the intensity of opposition is decreasing. An analysis of marriage polling numbers released on July 27, 2011, by poll- sters Joel Benenson from the Benenson Strategy Group and Jan van Lohuizen from Voter Consumer Research revealed that their "survey of historical data shows that intensity of opinion is shifting as well. Where previously opponents of marriage for same-sex couples held their views more strongly than marriage supporters, this is no longer the case. Support has not just grown, it has intensified as well." For example, the ABC News/*Washington Post* poll showed that "strong" support for gay marriage had increased by twelve points since 2004, while "strong" opposition had dropped by thirteen points. Since 2004, Pew's "strongly favor" numbers were up by twelve points; the "strongly oppose" side was down ten points. The authors say that supporters now equal marriage opponents in their intensity of support. They also conclude that Americans are in the process of rethinking their views on the issue and that this support for same-sex marriage will sharply increase in the coming years, particularly because of the overwhelming support for it among younger Americans. . . .

It should be clear to even die-hard opponents that public opinion on this issue has changed quicker than anyone imag- ined and that support will only grow, given the differences in opinion between young and old. No one can now credibly ar- gue that the courts or state legislatures are "imposing" same- sex marriage on an unwilling majority.

Four Decades of LGBT Activism Paved the Way for Marriage Equality

Freedom to Marry

Freedom to Marry is a nonprofit advocacy organization that works to end marriage discrimination in the United States.

For the past forty years, serious conversation and debate has surrounded the freedom to marry in the United States. The story of the freedom to marry has its intense ups and its devastating downs, but throughout it all, the discussion has been rooted in the desire for same-sex couples to express their love and commitment to each other in the same way that different-sex couples do: through marriage.

This timeline demonstrates the progress that the freedom to marry has experienced over the past 40 years, outlining the setbacks and celebrating the triumphs that same-sex couples have experienced. . . .

October 10, 1972: The U.S. Supreme Court dismisses *Baker v. Nelson*, one of three cases brought by same-sex couples, challenging the denial of marriage. . . . The U.S. Supreme Court summarily affirmed a ruling now long since superseded by progress, legal developments, and greater understanding of gay people and why marriage matters.

January 1, 1973: Maryland becomes the first state to pass a statute banning marriage between same-sex couples. . . . In waves of political attacks to block the freedom to marry in the 1990s and 2000s, numerous other states in the country pass similarly restrictive statutes. . . .

May 5, 1993: The Hawaii Supreme Court rules in *Baehr v. Lewin* that denying marriage to same-sex couples violates the Equal Protection Clause of the Hawaii Constitution.... The 1993 ruling means that if the state cannot show sufficient justification for its denial of the freedom to marry, the ban would be overturned.

The Defense of Marriage Act

September 21, 1996: President Bill Clinton signs the so-called Defense of Marriage Act (DOMA) into law. DOMA mandates unequal treatment of legally married same-sex couples, selectively depriving them of the 1,138+ protections and responsibilities that marriage triggers at the federal level....

November 3, 1998: Anti-gay forces succeed in amending the Hawaii Constitution to prevent the courts from ending the exclusion of same-sex couples.... On the same day, anti-gay forces in Alaska pass Ballot Measure 2, which amends the state constitution to restrict marriage to different-sex couples.

September 22, 1999: California becomes the first state to create a domestic partnership statute, allowing same-sex couples to receive some, but not all, of the protections afforded by marriage....

[On May 17, 2004] Massachusetts [became] the first state in the United States to allow same-sex couples to share in the freedom to marry.

December 20, 1999: The Vermont Supreme Court rules in *Baker v. State of Vermont* that same-sex couples must be treated equally to different-sex married couples. The Vermont legislature responds by establishing civil union, a separate legal status that affords couples some, but not all, of the protections that come with marriage—falling short of the constitutional command of equality, but far more than gay couples have had before. The law goes into effect on July 1, 2000.

November 7, 2000: Anti-gay forces in Nebraska push through the discriminatory Initiative Measure 416 at the ballot, constitutionally prohibiting the state from respecting any form of family status or recognition for same-sex couples. In the years that follow, similar amendments are passed in 27 additional states, writing marriage discrimination into a total of 29 state constitutions and disadvantaging millions of same-sex couples across the country.

November 18, 2003: The Massachusetts Supreme Court rules in *Goodridge v. Department of Public Health* that the state constitution mandates the freedom to marry for same-sex couples. Three months later, the Court reaffirms its decision, stating that only marriage—not separate and lesser mechanisms, such as civil union—sufficiently protects same-sex couples and their families.

May 17, 2004: Massachusetts becomes the first state in the United States to allow same-sex couples to share in the freedom to marry. Marriage opponents attempt to amend the constitution to strip away the freedom to marry, but the amendment is defeated on June 14, 2007, when over 75 percent of the state legislature votes to stand up for all families.

November 2, 2004: Anti-gay forces in eleven states, marshaled by Karl Rove, push through constitutional amendments to deny same-sex couples the freedom to marry. In Mississippi, Montana, and Oregon the amendments restrict marriage to different-sex couples. In the other states—Arkansas, Georgia, Kentucky, Michigan, North Dakota, Oklahoma, Ohio, and Utah—the amendments deny all forms of family recognition or status, including civil union and domestic partnership. A similar amendment banning marriage was passed in Missouri in August 2004.

January 19, 2005: The Louisiana Supreme Court reinstates a hurtful anti-family ban on marriage between same-sex couples, bringing the number of states with constitutional amendments against marriage to 17. . . .

April 20, 2005: Connecticut Governor Jodi Rell signs a civil union bill into law, affording same-sex couples some—but not all—of the projections that marriage provides. The law goes into effect on October 1, 2005.

California's Landmark Attempt

September 6, 2005: The California legislature becomes the first state legislature to pass a freedom to marry bill. The landmark bill is vetoed soon after passage by Governor Arnold Schwarzenegger. Two years later, the legislature again passes a marriage bill, and again, it is vetoed by Gov. Schwarzenegger.

November 8, 2005: The discriminatory constitutional amendment Proposition 2 is passed in Texas, constitutionally excluding same-sex couples from marriage. In April of that year, same-sex couples in Kansas are denied any form of family recognition by a similar anti-gay constitutional amendment.

October 25, 2006: The New Jersey Supreme Court issues a unanimous ruling in *Lewis v. Harris* that same-sex couples are entitled to all state-level spousal rights and responsibilities. . . . In December, the legislature fails to provide the full freedom to marry, settling for the creation of the separate and lesser mechanism of civil union.

The California Supreme Court [determined] in In Re: Marriage Cases *that a state statute excluding same-sex couples from marriage is unconstitutional.*

November 7, 2006: Anti-gay activists continue their anti-marriage, anti-family agenda by passing constitutional amendments denying same-sex couples the freedom to marry in seven more states—Colorado, Idaho, South Carolina, South

Dakota, Tennessee, Virginia, and Wisconsin. Arizona becomes the first state to reject an anti-gay marriage amendment at the ballot.

April 21, 2007: Washington state Governor Christine Gregoire signs a domestic partnership bill into law. In the weeks that follow, Oregon Governor Ted Kulongski and New Hampshire Governor John Lynch also sign a domestic partnership law and a civil union law, respectively. The laws [are all enacted].

May 15, 2008: The California Supreme Court determines in *In Re: Marriage Cases* that a state statute excluding same-sex couples from marriage is unconstitutional. Almost immediately, an initiative to overturn the court ruling (Proposition 8) qualifies for the November 2008 ballot. Same-sex couples begin marrying on June 16.

May 22, 2008: Maryland Governor Martin O'Malley signs into law a domestic partnership bill allowing same-sex couples in Maryland some—but not all—of the benefits that marriage affords. The law takes effect on July 1.

October 10, 2008: The Connecticut Supreme Court rules in *Kerrigan v. Commissioner of Public Health*, a case brought by Gay & Lesbian Advocates & Defenders, that same-sex couples are entitled to the freedom to marry. The law retroactively takes effect on October 1, allowing all couples the freedom to marry and converting existing civil unions between same-sex couples in the state into marriages.

November 4, 2008: Anti-gay forces push through Proposition 8 [in California], an anti-gay constitutional amendment that strips away same-sex couples' freedom to marry and restricts marriage to different-sex couples. Similar amendments are passed in Florida and Arizona.

April 3, 2009: The Iowa Supreme Court hands down a unanimous decision in favor of the freedom to marry in *Varnum v. Brien*. The ruling goes into effect on April 27, and same-sex couples begin marrying.

April 7, 2009: Vermont pushes past civil union and embraces the freedom to marry when the state legislature overwhelmingly votes to override a veto from Governor Jim Douglas. Same-sex couples begin applying for marriage licenses on September 1.

May 6, 2009: Maine Governor John Baldacci signs a freedom to marry bill into law previously approved by the state Senate and House of Representatives. Almost immediately, anti-gay activists work to push a ballot measure that would overturn the freedom to marry.

May 26 2009: The California Supreme Court rules that, notwithstanding Prop 8, marriages between same-sex couples that occurred in the four months between June and November remain valid.

Momentum for Marriage

May 31, 2009: Nevada approves a broad domestic partnership bill after the state legislature overrides a veto from the state's governor. Later that summer, Wisconsin also approves a less expansive domestic partnership bill.

[On July 8, 2010] U.S. District Court Judge Joseph Tauro *[ruled] in* Gill v. Office of Personnel Management *and* Commonwealth of Massachusetts v. United States Department of Health and Human Services *that DOMA's Section 3, which restricts marriage to different-sex couples, is unconstitutional.*

June 3, 2009: New Hampshire Governor John Lynch signs into law a freedom to marry bill approved by the state Senate and House of Representatives. The law takes effect on January 1, 2010.

November 3, 2009: Anti-gay forces in Maine push through an anti-gay ballot measure to overturn the freedom to marry in the state and restrict marriage to different-sex couples.

December 18, 2009: District of Columbia Mayor Adrian Fenty signs a freedom to marry bill into law after it passes by a large majority of City Council members. The law takes effect on March 3, 2010.

July 8, 2010: U.S. District Court Judge Joseph Tauro rules in *Gill v. Office of Personnel Management* and *Commonwealth of Massachusetts v. United States Department of Health and Human Services* that DOMA's Section 3, which restricts marriage to different-sex couples, is unconstitutional.

August 2010: CNN releases the first poll to show a national majority supporting the freedom to marry.

August 4, 2010: The U.S. District Court of Northern California declares that Proposition 8 violates the U.S. Constitution's due process and equal protection clauses, finding it unconstitutional to exclude same-sex couples from marriage. The case is appealed to the U.S. Ninth Circuit Court of Appeals.

January 31, 2011: Illinois Governor Pat Quinn signs a civil union bill into law after it is approved by the state Senate and House of Representatives. Later in 2011, civil union laws are also approved in Hawaii, Delaware, and Rhode Island.

February 23, 2011: President Barack Obama and Attorney General Eric Holder declare that because it is indefensible under the constitutional command of equal protection, the Administration will no longer defend the so-called Defense of Marriage Act. In a number of challenges to DOMA, the Obama Administration files briefs detailing and repudiating the history of government discrimination brought on by the unconstitutional DOMA.

March 16, 2011: The Respect for Marriage Act . . . , the bill that would overturn the so-called Defense of Marriage Act, is introduced. As of September 2012, the bill is supported by 156 cosponsors in the House and 33 in the Senate. . . .

June 24, 2011: New York Governor Andrew Cuomo signs a freedom to marry bill into law, more than doubling the number of Americans living in a state with the freedom to marry. . . . Couples begin marrying on July 24, 2011.

January 26, 2012: The Maine Freedom to Marry Coalition delivers more than 105,000 signatures to the Secretary of State to place a citizen's initiative on the November 2012 ballot. The measure would allow same-sex couples to receive a marriage license while also protecting religious freedom. Maine is the first state to proactively seek to win the freedom to marry at the ballot.

[On February 13, 2012] Washington Governor Christine Gregoire [signed] the freedom to marry into law after the state Senate and House approve it.

The Respect for Marriage Coalition

February 2, 2012: Freedom to Marry and the Human Rights Campaign team up to launch the Respect for Marriage Coalition, a group of over 50 civil rights, labor, progressive, faith, student, women's, and LGBT organizations dedicated to repealing the so-called Defense of Marriage Act.

February 7, 2012: The U.S. Ninth Circuit Court of Appeals upholds the August 4 ruling that found that Proposition 8 in California violates the U.S. Constitution. Anti-gay marriage advocates petition for an en banc hearing, requesting that 11 judges from the Court hear the case.

February 13, 2012: Washington Governor Christine Gregoire signs the freedom to marry into law after the state Senate and House approve it. Almost immediately after its passage, anti-gay activists begin collecting signatures to place a measure on the November ballot that would overturn the new law. The law was set to take effect on June 7, but anti-gay activists managed to collect enough signatures to put a stay on the law until November.

February 16, 2012: The New Jersey legislature approves the freedom to marry, but soon after, New Jersey Governor Chris Christie vetoes the bill. Freedom to Marry and local advocates are now working to build support in the legislature in order to override the veto, just as in Vermont in 2009.

February 22, 2012: U.S. District Court Judge Jeffrey White rules in *Golinski v. Office of Personnel Management*, declaring that DOMA's Section 3, which restricts marriage to different-sex couples, is unconstitutional. The cases [were] submitted for consideration by the U.S. Supreme Court.

March 1, 2012: Maryland Governor Martin O'Malley signs the freedom to marry into law. . . . [The law took] effect on January 1, 2013.

May 8, 2012: Anti-gay forces in North Carolina manage to pass a constitutional amendment that excludes same-sex couples from all forms of family status.

May 9, 2012: President Barack Obama becomes the first sitting president in the United States to publicly announce support for the freedom to marry. . . .

[On September 4, 2012, the] Democratic Party [became] the first major U.S. political party in history to officially endorse the freedom to marry in their national party platform when the platform is ratified at the Democratic National Convention.

Several DOMA Decisions

May 24, 2012: U.S. District Judge Claudia Wilken finds the Defense of Marriage Act unconstitutional in *Dragovich v. U.S. Department of Treasury*.

May 31, 2012: The U.S. First Circuit Court of Appeals finds the Defense of Marriage Act unconstitutional in two cases.

June 5, 2012: The full U.S. Court of Appeals for the Ninth Circuit denies anti-gay activists' petition for an en banc rehearing of the Proposition 8 case. The denial of the petition means that the Court's decision from February 2012, which found Prop. 8 to be unconstitutional, will stand. The case [was] submitted for consideration by the U.S. Supreme Court.

June 6, 2012: In New York, U.S. District Court Judge Barbara Jones finds the Defense of Marriage Act unconstitutional in *Windsor v. United States.* Judge Jones is the fifth federal judge to rule that DOMA's Section 3 violates the U.S. Constitution. The case [was] submitted for consideration by the U.S. Supreme Court.

July 31, 2012: In Connecticut, U.S. District Court Judge Vanessa Bryant finds the Defense of Marriage Act unconstitutional in *Pedersen v. Office of Personnel Management.* The case [was] submitted for consideration by the U.S. Supreme Court.

September 4, 2012: The Democratic Party becomes the first major U.S. political party in history to officially endorse the freedom to marry in their national party platform when the platform is ratified at the Democratic National Convention. . . .

November 6, 2012: On Election Day 2012, the freedom to marry triumphs at the ballot in all four states where it is up for a vote: Maine, Maryland, Minnesota, and Washington. In Maine, Maryland, and Washington, voters choose to end the exclusion of same-sex couples from marriage. In Minnesota, voters reject a hideous anti-gay constitutional amendment that would have permanently limited the freedom to marry in the state. President Barack Obama wins reelection, becoming the first president ever to run on a national party platform that fully and explicitly supports marriage for same-sex couples. And in a number of other races, pro-marriage legislatures were secured and pro-marriage judicial voices were retained. The freedom to marry takes effect in Washington on December 3, in Maine on December 29, and in Maryland on January 1, 2013.

December 7, 2012: The U.S. Supreme Court announces that it will hear two marriage cases at the federal level—*Windsor v. United States*, which takes on DOMA, and *Hollingsworth v. Perry*, which challenges California's Proposition 8. . . .

March 18, 2013: A new national poll demonstrates record support for the freedom to marry, with 58% of Americans saying they support marriage for same-sex couples.

March 26–27, 2013: The United States Supreme Court hears oral arguments in two landmark marriage cases: *Hollingsworth v. Perry*, the challenge to California's Proposition 8, and *Windsor v. United States*, a challenge to the so-called Defense of Marriage Act.

April 4, 2013: For the first time ever, a majority of United States Senators publicly support the freedom to marry. The landmark 51st announcement (from FL Senator Bill Nelson) ended a two-week period where over a dozen U.S. Senators—including two Republicans—announced that they support ending the exclusion of same-sex couples from marriage.

The Supreme Court's historic decisions will dramatically improve the lives of same-sex couples across the country, allowing many couples the ability to protect each other and their families.

April 24, 2013: Rhode Island Governor Lincoln Chafee signs a freedom to marry bill into law hours after it is approved by the Rhode Island Senate. The bill had already been approved overwhelmingly by the RI House. The freedom to marry [took] effect in the state on August 1, 2013.

May 7, 2013: Delaware Governor Jack Markell signs a freedom to marry bill into law immediately after it is approved by the Delaware Senate. The freedom to marry [took] effect in the state on July 1, 2013.

May 14, 2013: Minnesota Governor Mark Dayton signs a freedom to marry bill into law after both houses of the Minnesota legislature overwhelmingly approve the marriage bill. The freedom to marry [took] effect on August 1, 2013.

A Landmark Day at Court

June 26, 2013: The Supreme Court of the United States announces its decisions in two landmark cases dealing with the freedom to marry, overturning Section 3 of the so-called Defense of Marriage Act and dismissing the challenge to Proposition 8, letting a lower court ruling stand and restoring the freedom to marry in California. The Supreme Court's historic decisions will dramatically improve the lives of same-sex couples across the country, allowing many couples the ability to protect each other and their families.

October 21, 2013: Same-sex couples begin marrying at midnight in New Jersey after a court ruling declaring the freedom to marry across the state. Just hours after weddings begin in NJ, Gov. Chris Christie drops his appeal, halting efforts to restrict marriage to different-sex couples. The freedom to marry is the law of the land, making NJ the 14th state where same-sex couples can marry.

November 13, 2013: Governor Neil Abercrombie signed the freedom to marry into law in Hawaii after a three-week Special Session where legislators discussed why marriage matters to same-sex couples and their families. At last, Hawaii has completed its 20-year journey on the freedom to marry. Same-sex couples [began] marrying in Illinois on December 2, 2013.

November 20, 2013: Governor Pat Quinn signed the freedom to marry into law in Illinois after it was approved earlier in the year by the Illinois Senate and House. Same-sex couples were scheduled to begin marrying in Illinois in June 2014, until a federal judge ruled in favor of the freedom to marry in February 2014, moving the start date in many Illinois counties earlier.

December 19, 2013: The New Mexico Supreme Court issued a landmark decision in a lawsuit seeking clarification on laws regarding the freedom to marry in the state. The ruling affirmed the freedom to marry in every county in the state, making New Mexico the 17th state where same-sex couples can marry. . . .

December 20, 2013: U.S. District Court Judge Robert J. Shelby issued a ruling declaring that laws prohibiting same-sex couples from marrying in Utah are unconstitutional, conflicting with the U.S. Constitution's guarantees of equal protection and due process under the law. The ruling took effect immediately, and same-sex couples began marrying that afternoon. In the weeks that followed, the state of Utah declared commitment to appealing the decision, seeking a stay on the ruling. On January 6, the U.S. Supreme Court issued a stay as the appeals court fast-tracks the case. The 1,300 couples who married in the three-week period will be respected as what they are—married—by the U.S. government, but the state of Utah has declared that the marriage licenses issued in its own state will NOT be respected. The case [is working] its way through the 10th Circuit Court of Appeals.

December 23, 2013: U.S. District Court Judge Timothy Black issued a ruling declaring that the state of Ohio must respect marriages between same-sex couples on death certificates issued by the state. The ruling, which found that Ohio laws banning same-sex couples from marrying are unconstitutional, applied only to the issuance of death certificates, but it signaled that the court believes that Ohio cannot pick and choose which marriages it will respect. The case has been appealed to the 6th Circuit Court of Appeals.

Recent Developments

January 14, 2014: U.S. District Court Judge Terence Kern issued a ruling in favor of the freedom to marry in Oklahoma, a tremendous step forward for same-sex couples in the state. The decision, which was immediately stayed, has been appealed to the 10th Circuit Court of Appeals.

February 12, 2014: U.S. District Court Judge John G. Heyburn II . . . issued a ruling in Kentucky ordering the state to respect the marriages of same-sex couples legally performed in other states. The ruling was finalized on February 27, with a 21-day stay issued the following day. On March 4, Attorney General Conway said he would not appeal the ruling, but almost immediately after his announcement, Gov. Steve Beshear said he would appeal to the 6th Circuit Court of Appeals with private counsel.

February 13, 2014: U.S. District Judge Arenda L. Wright Allen issued a ruling in Virginia in favor of the freedom to marry for same-sex couples. The decision, which was immediately stayed, has been appealed to the 4th Circuit Court of Appeals, although Gov. McAuliffe and the Virginia Attorney General have said they will not defend anti-marriage laws.

February 26, 2014: U.S. District Judge Orlando Garcia issued a ruling in Texas in favor of the freedom to marry for same-sex couples. The decision, which was immediately stayed, has been appealed to the 5th Circuit Court of Appeals.

March 5, 2014: A new national poll tracks 59% support for the freedom to marry, a record high. The poll also is the first to demonstrate support at 50% or higher in every region of the country, plus broad support from both parties, with 40% support for marriage among Republicans.

American Politics Have Shifted Significantly Since the 1990s

Garance Franke-Ruta

Garance Franke-Ruta is the politics editor of The Atlantic Online. *Previously she was a national web politics editor for* The Washington Post.

Nineteen ninety-eight was a watershed year in the battle for gay rights in America—in a bad way. [U.S. President] Bill Clinton had in 1997 nominated James C. Hormel as ambassador to Luxembourg. But his nomination as the first openly gay U.S. ambassador stalled the following summer. Hormel, born during the early 1930s, had been a dean at the University of Chicago Law School and also a leader in creating gay institutions in his home town of San Francisco. In 1991, he endowed the Gay and Lesbian Center at the San Francisco Public Library, which would go on to bear his name when it opened.

His nomination snagged on the Republican leadership in Congress, then busily seeking President Clinton's impeachment over his affair with Monica Lewinsky. An even bigger obstacle was their disgust over Hormel's homosexuality.

Senator Jesse Helms, the Senate Foreign Relations Committee chairman well known for his public opposition to the "homosexual lifestyle" and the people he called, in *Newsweek* in 1994, "degenerates" and "weak, morally sick wretches," vowed to block the appointment. Senate Majority Leader Trent Lott of Mississippi on June 15, 1998, added fuel to the fire, comparing being gay to a condition "just like alcohol . . . or sex addiction . . . or kleptomania"—a pathology in need of treatment. House Majority Leader Dick Armey chimed in to support Lott, affirming, "The Bible is very clear on this." Assistant Senate Majority Leader Don Nickles of Oklahoma told "Fox News Sunday" on June 21, 1998, that Hormel "has promoted a lifestyle and promoted it in a big way, in a way that is very offensive." Against that backdrop, the comments of Republican Chuck Hagel, U.S. senator from Nebraska, didn't stand out as idiosyncratic. Ambassadors "are representing our lifestyle, our values, our standards. And I think it is an inhibiting factor to be gay—openly aggressively gay like Mr. Hormel—to do an effective job," Hagel, a member of the Senate Foreign Relations Committee, said after meeting with Hormel, according to a July 3, 1998 *Omaha-World Herald* story.

America is a different country now. But the "Stone Age" . . . , in which gay people were seen as perverts justifiably targeted for violence or invective, is a none too distant memory.

In September of that year, *Salon* revealed that House Judiciary Committee Chairman Henry Hyde—who had helped rush the Defense of Marriage Act [DOMA] through in 1996 as part of the Gingrich Revolution with the justification that same-sex unions were "illegitimate" and "immoral"—had broken up another man's marriage by having an affair with his wife. ([Then-speaker of the US House of Representatives] Newt Gingrich, who worked to push DOMA through and impeach the adulterous president who'd signed it, was later revealed to have also been having an affair at the time.)

In October 1998, 21-year-old gay University of Wyoming student Matthew Shepard was beaten into a coma and tied to a fence outside Laramie, [Wy.] where he would not be discovered for 18 hours. The passing motorist who discovered him at first thought he was a scarecrow, Reuters reported at the time. Shepard, whose skull had been cracked, never regained consciousness and died several days later at the Poudre Valley Hospital in Fort Collins, Colorado, from his severe injuries.

"A Different Country Now"

America is a different country now, a dozen years on from what Frank Rich described in 1999 as "[t]he homophobic epidemic of '98, which spiked with the October murder of Matthew Shepard."

After a decade of legislative fighting, federal hate crimes legislation was finally extended to protect gay people in 2009. The Matthew Shepard and James Byrd, Jr. Hate Crimes Prevention Act passed as a rider to the National Defense Reauthorization Act and was signed into law by President [Barack] Obama during his first year in office.

The president has done an "It Gets Better" video; so too have the White House staff and some leading Democrats in the United States Senate. Gay marriage is legal in nine states and the District of Columbia [at the time this article was written]; "Don't ask, don't tell" has been overturned; America has elected its first openly lesbian U.S. Senator—and from the Midwest!—and even the president backs same-sex marriage rights.

America is a different country now. But the "Stone Age," as [actress] Jodie Foster has called it, in which gay people were seen as perverts justifiably targeted for violence or invective, is a none too distant memory, and in too many quarters it is still extremely difficult for people—especially very young people—to be out and gay without experiencing severe social, physical, or economic repercussions (as the documentary *Bully* showed this past year [2013], in case any one had any doubt).

Today, according to *Washington Post*-ABC News polling, 58 percent support gay marriage, up from 41 percent in 2004, while opposition has dropped from 55 to 36 percent. A March

CNN/ORC International survey puts the jump as an increase from 40 to 56 percent support from 2007 through 2013.

And so the question arises: How does America address its homophobic past as it moves forward into a more tolerant future? If American views on gays have changed—and they have, with shocking rapidity—that means there are a lot of people in this country who used to hold more deeply anti-gay views than they do today, and who may be ashamed of what they once thought and said in what now seems a distant and unenlightened era. Two thirds of the change in views on gay marriage comes from "individuals' modifying their views over time" and only "one-third was due to a cohort succession effect, or later cohorts replacing earlier ones," according to sociologist Dawn Michelle Baunach, who looked into the issue in a 2011 *Social Science Quarterly* piece. Most such people have had the privilege of a private life, where their participation in an ugly ideology that diminished and damaged gay people is something they speak of only in conversation with friends, or recall within the inmost sanctuary of their own thoughts.

But some people have been living public lives a long time, and have left a very public paper trail of their expressions of discomfort and distaste. What is the proper response to the discovery of such information?

The moves by politicians on gay questions in the past year—and especially over the past three and a half months—have been by turns cautious and bold, awkwardly and imperfectly executed.

How do we as a society react when people openly change their views in public on gays, and on same-sex marriage?

And are we finally ready to get beyond the politics of the mid-1990s?

The Evolution of Politicians

The moves by politicians on gay questions in the past year—and especially over the past three and a half months—have been by turns cautious and bold, awkwardly and imperfectly executed. Some announcements were made under duress, or in haste, while others came seemingly out of the blue, fueled by paternal love or a sense of the historic moment. Not one of these pronouncements has escaped some measure of suspicion and derision by gay-rights activists or progressive writers, even as organized gay-rights groups have hailed them. (Few public comings out by gay public figures escape similar controversies.) But with the Supreme Court in June set to render decisions on the historic challenges to California's Proposition 8 banning same-sex marriage and the 1996 Defense of Marriage Act, which prohibits federal recognition of same-sex marriages permitted by the states, it's worth taking a look at how politicians have publicly "evolved," to use Obama's term, on the question of gay rights in America—and what, precisely, they have been evolving on.

Though the drumbeat of shifting views on gay marriage picked up in March [2013], thanks to the impending oral arguments in the Supreme Court cases, in many ways it was Hagel's January nomination to be defense secretary that began the conversation, and which gets at the core of the issue.

Gay money flooded into Obama's campaign coffers after he came out for gay marriage in May 2012—but gays and lesbians were also some of his staunched backers before that. A CNN analysis found one in 16 of his bundlers—high dollar fundraisers—in the first quarter of 2012 was gay; the *Advocate* estimated the number at closer to one in five in mid-2011, and the *Washington Post* at one in six in May 2012.

Gay voters went on to reveal they had some serious clout at the polls in November. "Mr. Obama's more than three-to-one edge in exit polls among the 5 percent of voters who identified themselves as gay, lesbian or bisexual was more than enough to give him the ultimate advantage," according to a *New York Times* post-election report analyzing the impact of the GLB vote (no T measured). The fact that Obama was able to win reelection after publicly backing gay marriage—and the tremendous debt he owed gay voters and political fundraisers—helped change dynamics in Washington around gay issues in the immediate post-election period.

A Growing Power Base

In particular, gay leaders who'd bit their tongues in advance of the election felt newly empowered to push back at the president, and the Hagel nomination provided an early opportunity to do that. Not only had Hagel spoken disparagingly of Hormel, but he had "a zero-per-cent rating (three times) from the Human Rights Campaign, the leading gay-rights lobby," according to Richard Socarides. "Among other things, Hagel voted against extending basic employment nondiscrimination protections and the federal hate-crimes law to cover gay Americans."

> *The Defense of Marriage Act was a very successful piece of legislation. . . . Between 1996—when DOMA was passed—and 2006, only one member of the U.S. Senate came out in support of same-sex marriage.*

Hagel was the man who would manage the oversight of the end of "Don't Ask, Don't Tell," as well as the winding down of the war in Afghanistan. His views, so common in 1998, were seen as bluntly prejudiced in 2013—and as such, anathema to both gay conservatives eager to tar a potential Obama nominee, and gay liberals infuriated that the reward for their electoral support would be the nomination of someone who talked like that about them.

Hagel recognized the severity of the situation and apologized before he was even nominated. "My remarks 14 years ago in 1998 were insensitive," he said in a statement. "They do not reflect my views or the totality of my public record, and I apologize to Ambassador Hormel and any L.G.B.T. Americans who may question my commitment to their civil rights. I am fully supportive of 'open service' and committed to L.G.B.T. military families." That tamped down criticism, but not fully, and not on the right.

Criticism of the administration erupted anew when it was revealed that the pastor selected to give the inaugural benediction had also made anti-gay remarks. "We must lovingly but firmly respond to the aggressive agenda of not all, but of many in the homosexual community," Louie Giglio had preached in the mid-90s, warning that gays were going to hell, and that they could change with the help of Jesus. When he declined to apologize, he was quietly dropped from the inaugural program. "Due to a message of mine that has surfaced from 15–20 years ago, it is likely that my participation, and the prayer I would offer, will be dwarfed by those seeking to make their agenda the focal point of the inauguration," he told ThinkProgress.

And it was progress. When in 2008 it was revealed that Rick Warren, the pastor selected to give Obama's 2009 inaugural invocation, had called homosexuality a sin (but "not the worst sin") and unnatural, he stayed on the program.

The Effect of DOMA

The Defense of Marriage Act was a very successful piece of legislation. Not only did it create two categories of marital benefits—one for straights, and one for gays—but it had a profound silencing effect on political leaders. Between 1996—when DOMA was passed—and 2006, only one member of the U.S. Senate came out in support of same-sex marriage, according to data collected by Wonkblog's Dylan Matthews: Dean Barkley of Minnesota, who replaced Paul Wellstone after his death in 2002 and served a grand total of 61 days in office.

But starting in 2012, that began to shift—thanks in large measure to Joe Biden.

The vice president got the ball rolling on the new round of gay-marriage pronouncements on May 6. "I am absolutely comfortable with the fact that men marrying men, women marrying women and heterosexual—men and women marrying—are entitled to the same exact rights, all the civil rights, all the civil liberties," he told NBC's *Meet the Press.* That put pressure on Obama to make his own views clearer—not that there was much doubt about what they were. "There's no doubt in my mind that the president shares these values and that's why it's time for him to speak out in favor of marriage equality as well," Joe Solmonese, president of the Human Rights Campaign, said in a statement. Days later, Obama sat down with ABC's Robin Roberts, telling her, "I've just concluded that, for me personally, it is important for me to go ahead and affirm that I think same-sex couples should be able to get married."

By the end of 2011, only 15 U.S. senators had endorsed same sex marriage. In 2013, so far, 19 senators have come out to support same sex marriage—including six just in the first week of April—as pressure from gay groups and the impending Supreme Court decision helped create a cascade effect. The evolution has been eased by the gay marriage movement's wins in state legislatures and ballot initiatives.

What's happening now is a wholesale repudiation of the 1990s move to eject gay people from the American family, writ large.

Family Experiences Change Hearts and Minds

The most important boulder to be unlodged was Republican Sen. Rob Portman, who changed his position two years after his son came out as gay and who is now out front ahead of the Ohio voters who elected him. His Op-Ed and his courage put pressure on Democratic hold-outs who shared his beliefs but were shy of expressing them.

Portman's shifting view was presented "absolutely perfectly," said Fred Sainz, a spokesman for the Human Rights Campaign. Many parents are not as supportive of their gay children as Portman has been, he pointed out. "I'm now 45 years old. I came out when I was 28. My father hasn't spoken to me since I came out. I would love to have a dad like Rob Portman," he told me. Wrote Will Portman of his coming out two years ago: "[my parents] were surprised to learn I was gay, and full of questions, but absolutely rock-solid supportive. That was the beginning of the end of feeling ashamed about who I was."

As if to emphasize the point, Republican Rep. Matt Salmon told a local TV station in Arizona in April that he wasn't going to budge on gay marriage despite having a gay son.

What's happening now is a wholesale repudiation of the 1990s move to eject gay people from the American family, writ large. The reason for DOMA was anti-gay animus by a group of men who showed their respect for marriage by divorcing multiple times and having affairs. The reason to undo DOMA is a rejection of that animus, and the growing recognition there is no way to argue against same-sex marriage that is not ultimately an argument for the moral inferiority of gay people. As of Friday, only four Democrats in the U.S. Senate had not come out in favor of gay marriage.

"I have concluded the federal government should no longer discriminate against people who want to make lifelong, loving commitments to each other or interfere in personal, private, and intimate relationships," Sen. Heidi Heitkamp of North Dakota said. "I view the ability of anyone to marry as a logical extension of this belief."

The reason to not support gay marriage is the lingering sense that there's something strange or not right about it. That it's fine for gay people to do what they want in privacy, but that their relationships are not the same as straight ones. Not as powerful, not as loving, not as legitimate.

"[T]his is the inevitable extension of my efforts to promote equality and opportunity for everyone," said Sen. Mark Warner in announcing his new views. "[A]s many of my gay and lesbian friends, colleagues and staff embrace long term committed relationships, I find myself unable to look them in the eye without honestly confronting this uncomfortable inequality," observed Senator Claire McCaskill in a Tumblr post.

Rejecting the Moralist

The 1990s are over. Newt Gingrich, who stepped down as House Speaker after the Republicans performed poorly at the polls in 1998, in 2012 lost his comeback bid and the Republican presidential primary. Former representative Bob Barr, the sponsor of DOMA in 1996, in 2009 recanted his support for the bill and said gays should be allowed to marry. Bill Clinton—who signed it the bill with a statement saying "I have long opposed governmental recognition of same-gender marriages"—has too.

But if that moment of moralism in the mid-90s deserves to be remembered, it's for the lesson that the American people, when they stop being upset about an issue, really let it go. Clinton was impeached over his infidelity, but he hung on to office and became one of the most beloved ex-presidents ever. His party even won seats in the House and Senate the same year his scandal dominated the news, as the public defied political predictions and turned against the moralists instead of the man they accused.

As the drumbeat of shifting views of gay marriage continues, each voice affirms gay people as part of the American family, and each senator freshly legitimizes gay Americans as he or she repudiates past views or clarifies new ones. . . . This moment of change and affirmation—this moment of public evolution—is having a power all its own.

Unequal Treatment Led the Supreme Court to Overturn DOMA

Adam Gabbatt

Adam Gabbatt is a New York city-based reporter and live blogger for the Guardian *newspaper.*

Edith Windsor and Thea Spyer were together for 40 years before they married in 2007. When Spyer died in 2009 Windsor, in the midst of her grief, was ordered to pay $363,000 in estate taxes as the federal government did not recognise the pair's marriage.

Windsor appealed, and won. The [U.S.] Supreme Court agreed to hear her challenge to the Defense of Marriage Act, or DOMA, in December [2012], a decision Windsor told the *Guardian* had left her "delirious with joy."

"I think DOMA is wrong for all of the various ways in which it discriminates against same-sex married couples and against gays all together," Windsor said. "It's enormously satisfying and fulfilling and exciting to be where we are now."

Spyer, she said, would have been proud of her achievement. "I think she'd be so proud and happy and just so pleased at how far we have come. It's a culmination of an engagement that happened between us in 1967 when we didn't dream that we'd be able to marry."

Windsor, now a snappily dressed 83-year-old who is rarely seen without a long string of pearls around her neck, seems to have easily slotted into her position as the public face of marriage equality. But it is a role which must have seemed hard to imagine when in her early 20s, the then Edith Schlain married Saul Windsor, a friend of her brother's. The two separated in 1952 after less than a year.

"I told him the truth," Windsor recalled in an interview with NPR [National Public Radio] this year. "I said: 'Honey, you deserve a lot more. You deserve somebody who thinks you're the best because you are. And I need something else.'"

On Her Own in the Big City

Windsor was born in Philadelphia in 1929, in the midst of the Depression. Her parents lost their home and business not long after her birth. In interviews she has recalled identifying with the leading men in the movies she went to watch while growing up, not the woman he was attempting to woo. Despite those feelings, she said she had no awareness of what life as a lesbian could be like.

"I could not imagine a life that way," she told Buzzfeed. "I wanted to be like everybody else. You marry a man who supports you—it never occurred to me I'd have to earn a living, and nor did I study to earn a living."

The divorce meant Windsor now had to do just that. She retained her name from the marriage but changed her life by moving to New York and concentrating on her career. Windsor worked as a secretary while studying at New York University [NYU]. When she graduated with a master's degree in mathematics she took a job at IBM.

Spyer proposed [to Windsor] in 1967, with a brooch rather than a ring—Windsor did not want to face questions from co-workers about the assumed husband-to-be.

Windsor said she would feel envious when she saw other women out together, but still found it hard to be openly gay in pre-Stonewall New York City. Finally, however, she decided she had had enough.

"About 1962, I suddenly couldn't take it any more," she recalled in *Edie & Thea: A Very Long Engagement,* a 2009 film made about her and Spyer's life and wedding.

"And I called an old friend of mine, a very good friend and I said if you know where the lesbians go please take me. Somebody brought Thea over and introduced her and we just started dancing."

That was in Portofino, a restaurant in Greenwich Village. The pair kept dancing until, as Windsor tells it, she got a hole in her stocking. They would go to parties, dancing all the while, for two years until they started dating. Spyer proposed in 1967, with a brooch rather than a ring—Windsor did not want to face questions from co-workers about the assumed husband-to-be.

A Love Affair for the Ages

"It was a love affair that just kept on and on and on," Windsor said. "It really was. Something like three weeks before Thea died she said: 'Jesus we're still in love, aren't we.'"

The couple moved into an apartment near Washington Square in Manhattan, where Windsor still lives, and bought a house together in Southampton, Long Island. Windsor rose to the highest technical position within IBM, and Spyer saw patients in their apartment. In the years following the Stonewall riots they both marched and demonstrated for equal rights.

In 1977, aged 45, Spyer was diagnosed with multiple sclerosis. They could still dance, Windsor told Buzzfeed, with Spyer ditching her crutches at the dance floor and leading with her good leg.

As Spyer's health deteriorated, Windsor eventually became her full-time care giver. Getting ready for bed could take an hour, preparing to leave the house in the morning three or four, she said in an interview with the NYU alumni magazine.

In 2007, Spyer's doctors told her she had one year left to live.

"Having gotten the bad prognosis she woke up the next morning and said: 'Do you still want to get married?'," Windsor said. "And I said 'Yes'. And she said: 'So do I.'"

The pair flew to Canada that year with six friends and were married in Toronto. Windsor wore white, Thea was in all black. The ceremony was officiated by Canada's first openly gay judge, justice Harvey Brownstone.

Marriage Makes a Difference

"Many people ask me why get married," Windsor said in remarks on the steps of the supreme court in March [2013], the day the court heard arguments in her case against DOMA.

"I was 77, Thea was 75, and maybe we were older than that at that point, but the fact is that everybody treated it as different. It turns out marriage is different."

Attorneys representing Windsor argued in the Supreme Court that DOMA violates the Constitution in not recognising her marriage to Spyer.

"I've asked a number of long-range couples, gay couples when they've got married, I've asked them: 'Was it different the next morning' and the answer is always: 'Yes. It's a huge difference.'"

Less than two years after they were married, Spyer died. A month after that, Windsor had a heart attack.

"In the midst of my grief I realised that the federal government was treating us as strangers, and it meant paying a humongous estate tax. And it meant selling a lot of stuff to do it and it wasn't easy. I live on a fixed income and it wasn't easy" she said.

Two lower courts had already ruled that it was unconstitutional for Windsor to have to pay the $363,000 in federal estate taxes. Attorneys representing Windsor argued in the Supreme Court that DOMA violates the Constitution in not recognising her marriage to Spyer.

When the *Guardian* spoke to Windsor back in December [2012], the day the the court agreed to hear her case, the joy in her voice was clear. She felt optimistic, too.

"I really believe in the Supreme Court. First of all, I'm the youngest in my family and justice matters a lot—the littlest one gets pushed around a lot. And I trust the Supreme Court, I trust the Constitution—so I feel a certain confidence that we'll win."

It turns out she was right. [The U.S. Supreme Court ruled in Windsor's favor on June 26, 2013, overturning key provisions of DOMA and paving the way for the federal government's recognition of same-sex marriages, which soon followed.]

State Marriage Laws Vary Widely Following DOMA's Demise

National Conference of State Legislatures

The National Conference of State Legislatures (NCSL) is a bipartisan nongovernmental organization established in 1975 to serve state legislatures around the country. All state legislators and staff members are automatically members of NCSL. The organization provides research, technical assistance, and opportunities for policy makers to exchange ideas on state issues and is an advocate for the interests of the states in the American federal system.

State legislatures and voters have made sweeping changes over the past two decades in laws defining whether marriage is limited to relationships between a man and a woman or is extended to same-sex couples. Thirty-three states currently define marriage as a relationship between a man and a woman and prohibit same-sex marriages, while seventeen states and the District of Columbia allow same-sex marriage. These contrasting state laws concerning same-sex marriage reflect sharp divergence in the views toward marriage and same-sex marriage across the country.

On March 21 [2014] a federal judge in Michigan ruled that state's ban on same-sex marriage is unconstitutional. This ruling joins with similar rulings in Virginia, Kentucky, Texas, Oklahoma and Utah. Shortly after the decision was made a stay was issued.

The New Mexico Supreme Court ruled on Dec. 19, 2013 that same-sex couples are allowed to marry. Before the ruling,

New Mexico was the only state without a law or constitutional provision explicitly banning or allowing same-sex marriage. Some county officials had issued marriage licenses to same-sex couples in previous years. After the U.S. Supreme Court [Defense of Marriage Act] ruling in June 2013, the state asked the New Mexico Supreme Court to make a decision regarding their state policy. The state Supreme Court heard arguments in October and ruled on Dec. 19, 2013, that same-sex couples in the state were allowed to marry. The ruling goes into effect immediately.

The New Mexico court ruling makes it eight states where same-sex marriages were made legal this year [2013], joining Hawaii, Illinois, Delaware, Minnesota, Rhode Island (all through legislation) and California and New Jersey (through court decisions).

Most states have adopted prohibitions of same-sex marriage.

States Are Strongly Divided on the Issue

States are strongly divided on same-sex marriage. Thirty-three states prohibit same-sex marriage, including 29 states that have prohibitions in their state constitutions. With New Mexico, 17 states along with the District of Columbia allow same-sex marriage. Most states that have recently allowed same-sex marriage have done so through legislation.

Since the beginning of 2011, eight states have passed legislation, one adopted it by initiative and three allow same-sex marriage as a result of court decisions. In six of the states that adopted same-sex marriage by legislation, they overturned previous statutes that prohibited same-sex marriage. (None of these states had constitutional provisions prohibiting same-sex marriage.)

The scope for continued legislative change is limited. Of the 33 states that do not allow same-sex marriage, 29 have constitutional provisions that require popular votes, usually alongside legislative action. Efforts to overturn constitutional prohibitions have begun in several states and litigation has also been initiated in several states. . . .

State legislatures have been deeply involved in the public debates about how to define marriage and whether the official recognition of "marriage" should be limited to relationships involving one man and one woman or that same-sex couples should also be entitled to "marriage." State legislatures have gone both ways in this debate: either enacting "defense of marriage" laws and constitutional provisions or, going the opposite direction, adopting laws allowing same sex marriage.

Most states have adopted prohibitions of same-sex marriage. Most states did so by adopting "defense of marriage" language that defines marriage in their state constitution and/or state law in a way similar to the language in the federal Defense of Marriage Act (DOMA)—"the word 'marriage' means only a legal union between one man and one woman as husband and wife." Other states prohibit same sex marriages or marriages between persons of the same sex or gender. Twenty-nine states have placed that language in their state constitutions (26 of these states also have statutory provisions adopting this language). A further four states have statutory language adopting the restrictive language.

A Litany of Legal Decisions

Seventeen states and the District of Columbia currently allow same-sex marriages. In New Mexico, Massachusetts, Connecticut, and Iowa, the courts ruled that the state constitution required that same-sex couples be accorded the same marriage rights as opposite-sex couples. In Vermont, New Hampshire, Connecticut (following the state court decision), the District of Columbia, New York, Maryland, Washington, Rhode Island

and Delaware legislative bodies have passed statutory changes that allow same-sex marriages. In Maine, the legislature passed a same-sex marriage law in 2009, which was repealed in a voter referendum. In 2012, Maine voters reversed course and approved a same-sex marriage statute.

The U.S. Supreme Court on June 26, 2013, declined to hear the appeal overruling California's Proposition 8, reinstating the federal district court decision allowing same-sex marriages. New Jersey's court decision to establish same-sex marriage took effect on October 21, 2013. Hawaii and Illinois adopted legislation late in 2013 to allow same-sex marriage. New Mexico's Supreme Court ruled on December 19, 2013 that same-sex couples in the state are allowed to marry. A federal judge in Utah ruled the state's ban on same-sex marriage to be unconstitutional in December 2013, but this case is pending appeal. Same-sex marriage is not allowed in Utah. The same is true in Oklahoma where a federal judge in January 2014 ruled the state's ban unconstitutional. The decision was immediately stayed pending appeal.

Divorces of same-sex marriages and dissolution of civil unions remain a challenge for same-sex couples in many states.

Several states have also expanded the legal rights available to spouses in same-sex relationships while also limiting marriage to opposite-sex couples with civil unions and domestic partnerships.

Four states allow civil unions available to both same-sex and opposite-sex couples. Civil unions provide legal recognition to the couple's relationship while providing legal rights to the partners similar to those accorded to spouses in marriages. Two states (Nevada and Oregon) have adopted broad domestic partnerships that grant nearly all state-level spousal rights to unmarried couples. In Nevada, domestic partnerships are available to both same-sex and opposite-sex couples.

Divorce Laws Are Complicated

Divorces of same-sex marriages and dissolution of civil unions remain a challenge for same-sex couples in many states. Divorce laws generally depend on the state or states of residence, rather than the state where the marriage was granted.

- Same-sex couples who live in a state where same-sex marriages are allowed may obtain a divorce according to the laws of that state, regardless of where the marriage was granted.

- Same-sex couples who are married or in civil unions and who live in states that allow civil unions can also dissolve their legal relationship. Colorado, Hawaii, Illinois and New Jersey allow civil unions.

- Same-sex couples living in states that do not allow same-sex marriages often cannot get divorced in their home state because the marriage is not recognized, even for the limited purpose of divorce. At least three states that do not allow same-sex marriage do allow divorces of resident same-sex couples: Arizona, New Mexico and Wyoming.

- Same-sex couples living in states that do not allow same-sex marriages usually cannot simply go back to the state where they married or another state that allows same-sex marriage to get a divorce. Residency requirements for divorce (often 90 days or longer) can make divorce impractical in the state where the couple was married.

Access to divorce for non-resident couples may be expanding. In the past two years, three states (Vermont, Delaware and Minnesota) and D.C. allow couples married in that state to get a divorce without having to meet the residency requirements that normally apply.

Young People Helped Shift Public Opinion on Same-Sex Marriage

Robert P. Jones, Daniel Cox, and Elizabeth Cook

Robert P. Jones is chief executive officer of the Public Religion Research Institute (PRRI), a nonpartisan nonprofit organization dedicated to researching the relationship between religion, values, and public life. Daniel Cox is the research director for PRRI, and Elizabeth Cook is a data analysis consultant for the organization.

Millennials (Americans age 18 to 29) are at the vanguard of the shift that is occurring on attitudes about gay and lesbian people and homosexuality. On basic questions of policy, views about gay and lesbian people in the church and in society, and moral judgments about homosexuality, Millennials are much more liberal than the general public and dramatically more so than seniors (Americans age 65 or older). It is difficult to find another issue on which there is deeper generational disagreement than on the issue of homosexuality and rights for gay and lesbian people.

On the issue of same-sex marriage, generational differences are striking, whether the context is public policy or church policy. More than 6-in-10 (62%) Millennials favor allowing gay and lesbian couples to marry legally, double the support found among seniors (31%). The generational differences also cut across partisan and religious lines. For instance, among Republicans overall, less than one-third (31%) favor same-sex marriage; however, nearly half (49%) of Republican

Millennials favor allowing gay and lesbian people to marry. Similarly, among white evangelical Protestants overall, less than 1-in-5 (19%) favor allowing gay and lesbian couples to marry, but 44% of white evangelical Millennials favor it.

Young people are also much more supportive of gay and lesbian people being allowed to serve as religious leaders. More than 6-in-10 (61%) say gay and lesbian people should be eligible for ordination with no special requirements, compared to about one-third (34%) of seniors. There is also broader acceptance of gay and lesbian relationships in general. Nearly 8-in-10 (77%) Millennials agree that gay and lesbian relationships should be accepted by society, while seniors are evenly divided (48% agree, 48% disagree).

Millennials are also far less critical in their moral evaluations of same-sex sexual relationships than seniors. Less than half (46%) of young people say that sex between two adults of the same gender is morally wrong, compared to 69% of seniors. Half of Millennials say that sex between two adults of the same gender is morally acceptable, a view held by only 26% of seniors. Millennials are also more accepting of premarital sex than older generations. However, they are as likely as seniors to say abortion is morally wrong. Nearly 6-in-10 (59%) Millennials and seniors say that abortion is morally wrong.

Attitude Changes on Same-Sex Marriage

Public attitudes about same-sex marriage have been steadily becoming more favorable over time. Within the last 5 years public support for same-sex marriage has increased significantly, with many polling organizations recording double-digit increases in support over this period. In 2011, for the first time, multiple surveys from different organizations (including Gallup, ABC/*Washington Post*, CNN and PRRI) found that a majority of the public favored same-sex marriage.

Polling from Public Religion Research Institute [PRRI] has confirmed the increase in support in 2011 compared to previous years, with a cluster of findings now showing about half or a small majority of Americans supporting same-sex marriage. In May 2011, PRRI found for the first time a slim majority (51%) favoring allowing gay and lesbian people to marry, compared to 43% opposing and 6% reporting they did not know. In the Millennials, Religion, and Gay/Lesbian Issues Survey in July 2011, 47% of the public report that they favor allowing gay and lesbian people to marry, 47% report they are opposed, and 6% report they do not know.

The Millennial generation is more supportive of public policies protecting rights of gay and lesbian Americans than older Americans.

The same shift in opinion on same-sex marriage evident in recent surveys is also found in Americans' self-reports of how their views have changed over the last 5 years. While most Americans' views have not changed significantly over this period, among the nearly 3-in-10 whose views have shifted, twice as many Americans say their views have become more supportive than more opposed. Nearly 1-in-5 (19%) Americans say they are more supportive of the legality of same-sex marriage than they were 5 years ago, compared to only 9% who say they are now more opposed.

Millennials (29%), Hispanics (25%), and Catholics (23%) are significantly more likely than the general public to say they have become more supportive of same-sex marriage over the last five years. Hispanics, however, are also more likely than the general public to say they have become more opposed (17%). Seniors are the only group who are more likely to say they have become more opposed (17%) than more supportive (12%).

The Millennial generation is more supportive of public policies protecting rights of gay and lesbian Americans than older Americans. The generational differences between Millennials and seniors are the greatest on the issue of same-sex marriage, but there is at least a 20-point generation gap on each policy measure included in the survey.

Religion Plays a Role

There are major religious groups on each side of the debate over allowing gay and lesbian couples to marry legally. On the one hand, majorities of religiously unaffiliated Americans (70%), Americans affiliated with a non-Christian religion (67%), Catholics (52%), and white mainline Protestants (51%) favor allowing gay and lesbian couples to marry legally. On the other hand, large majorities of white evangelical Protestants and African American Protestants are opposed. Approximately three-quarters (76%) of white evangelical Protestants oppose allowing gay and lesbian couples to marry, including nearly half (47%) who strongly oppose it. Six-in-ten African American Protestants oppose allowing gay and lesbian couples to marry, including 42% who strongly oppose.

Frequency of religious attendance is strongly correlated with support for same-sex marriage, but the attendance patterns matter somewhat more for Protestants than for Catholics. Nearly half (47%) of Protestants report attending services weekly or more, 36% report attending monthly or a few times per year, and 16% report attending seldom or never. Protestants who attend religious services weekly or more strongly oppose allowing gay and lesbian people to marry (77% oppose, 19% favor). Compared to weekly or more attenders, more than twice as many Protestants who attend monthly or a few times a year (44%) and Protestants who seldom or never attend (49%) favor allowing gay and lesbian couples to marry. The support gap between Protestants who attend weekly or more and those who attend once or twice a month or a few times a year is a striking 25 points.

Slightly fewer (41%) Catholics than Protestants report attending religious services weekly or more, 40% report attending monthly or a few times a year, and 18% report attending seldom or never. The religious attendance affect is more muted among Catholics. Among Catholics who attend religious services weekly or more, 43% support allowing gay and lesbian couples to marry. Fully 6-in-10 (60%) Catholics who attend religious services monthly or a few times a year support same-sex marriage, as do similar numbers of Catholics who seldom or never attend (55%). The support gap between Catholics who attend weekly or more and those who attend monthly or a few times a year is 17 points.

Support for same-sex marriage is positively correlated with higher education levels.

Demographic Differences

Women are more supportive of same-sex marriage than men, with 51% of women and only 41% of men in favor of allowing gay and lesbian couples to marry. The differences are greatest between the sexes on intensity of support. Twenty-two percent of women, compared to only 13% of men, say they strongly favor allowing gay and lesbian couples to marry. Gender differences also persist within the Millennial generation. For example, about one-third (34%) of Millennial females strongly favor allowing gay and lesbian couples to marry, compared to just over 1-in-5 (22%) of their male counterparts.

Support for same-sex marriage is positively correlated with higher education levels. Among those with the least education (high school or less), only 36% support allowing gay and lesbian couples to marry. In contrast, majorities of those with a college degree (55%) and those with post-graduate education (63%) support allowing gay and lesbian couples to marry.

Democrats are much more supportive of same-sex marriage than Republicans, with those identifying as Independents closely mirroring the general public. Nearly 6-in-10 (58%) Democrats, 47% of Independents, and only 31% of Republicans favor allowing gay and lesbian couples to marry. Nearly 4-in-10 (37%) Republicans are strongly opposed to same-sex marriage.

About 15% of Americans say they consider themselves part of the Tea Party movement. Those identifying with the Tea Party are more opposed to same-sex marriage than other Americans, including Americans who identify as Republican. About two-thirds (68%) of self-identified Tea Party members oppose same-sex marriage, including 42% who are strongly opposed.

Civil Unions

More than 6-in-10 (62%) Americans say they favor "allowing gay and lesbian couples to enter into legal agreements with each other that would give them many of the same rights as married couples," and about 1-in-4 (26%) do so strongly. Seven-in-ten Americans who support civil unions also support same-sex marriage.

Younger and older Americans approach the issues of same-sex marriage and civil unions differently. Among the Millennial generation, support for civil unions (71%) is only 9 points higher than support for same-sex marriage (62%). Among seniors, there is a 20-point difference in support levels for the two policies. A majority (51%) of seniors favor civil unions, but less than one-third (31%) favor allowing gay and lesbian couples to marry.

Strong majorities of Americans in every major religious group except white evangelicals and black Protestants support civil unions. Approximately 8-in-10 religiously unaffiliated

Americans (78%) and non-Christian religiously affiliated Americans (80%) support civil unions, as do approximately 7-in-10 white mainline Protestants (71%) and Catholics (69%). On the other hand, only 48% of black Protestants and only 39% of white evangelical Protestants support civil unions, and majorities of each oppose them (52% and 58% respectively).

Gay Marriage Around the World

David Masci, Elizabeth Sciupac, and Michael Lipka

David Masci is a senior researcher at the Pew Research Center, a nonpartisan, nonprofit research organization. Elizabeth Sciupac is a research analyst and Michael Lipka is an assistant editor at the Pew Research Center.

A growing number of governments around the world are considering whether to grant legal recognition to same-sex marriages. More than a dozen countries currently have national laws allowing gays and lesbians to marry, mostly in Europe and the Americas. In two other countries, including the United States, some jurisdictions allow same-sex couples to wed, while others do not.

Countries That Allow Gay Marriage

Scotland (2014)

On Feb. 4, 2014, the Scottish Parliament (known as the Holyrood) voted overwhelmingly to approve legislation legalizing same-sex marriage. In addition to allowing same-sex couples to wed, the measure gives churches and other religious groups the option of deciding whether or not they want to conduct such marriages. The two largest churches in Scotland—the Church of Scotland and the Roman Catholic Church—oppose same-sex marriage and lobbied against the bill in the Holyrood.

As Scotland is a semi-autonomous part of the United Kingdom (UK), the law will not take effect until the UK's national parliament in London passes enacting legislation. But given that the national parliament already legalized same-sex marriage in England and Wales (see next entry), the passage of such enacting legislation is considered a formality. Same-sex couples are expected to be able to wed in Scotland as early as the fall of 2014.

England and Wales (2013)

On July 17, 2013, Queen Elizabeth II gave her "royal assent" to a bill legalizing same-sex marriage in England and Wales. The day before, the measure had won final passage in the British Parliament after months of debate. The law only applies to England and Wales because Scotland and Northern Ireland are semi-autonomous and have separate legislative bodies to decide many domestic issues, including the definition of marriage. While Northern Ireland's legislature in April 2013 voted down a measure that would have legalized same-sex marriage, the Scottish Parliament passed a bill to legalize same-sex marriage in February 2014.

The new law in England and Wales, which was a priority for British Prime Minister and Conservative Party leader David Cameron, allows gay and lesbian couples to marry beginning March 29, 2014. However, the law prohibits same-sex weddings within the Church of England, which continues to define marriage as between one man and one woman.

Brazil (2013)

On May 14, 2013, Brazil's National Council of Justice ruled that same-sex couples should not be denied marriage licenses, allowing same-sex marriages to begin nationwide. (Previously, about half of Brazil's 27 jurisdictions had allowed same-sex marriage.)

The conservative Social Christian Party has appealed the Council of Justice's decision to the Supreme Court, and Brazil's legislature may still weigh in on the issue, leaving some uncertainty surrounding the future of same-sex marriage in the world's fifth-largest country.

France (2013)

On May 18, French President Francois Hollande signed into law a measure legalizing same-sex marriage, making France the 14th country to grant gays and lesbians the right to wed. Although the bill had passed the National Assembly and the Senate in April, Hollande's signature had to wait until a court challenge brought by the conservative opposition party, the UMP, was resolved. On May 17, France's highest court, the Constitutional Council, ruled that the bill was constitutional.

[France has] pushed through a law that not only legalizes same-sex marriage but also gives gay and lesbian couples the right to adopt children—a provision that has drawn especially strong criticism from French Catholic leaders.

In May 2012, Hollande was elected and his Socialist Party won majorities in both houses of France's legislature. True to their campaign promises, Hollande and the Socialists have pushed through a law that not only legalizes same-sex marriage but also gives gay and lesbian couples the right to adopt children—a provision that has drawn especially strong criticism from French Catholic leaders.

While recent polls show that a majority of French adults support the law, opposition to the change has been intense. Since the beginning of 2013, several anti-gay marriage protests with occasionally volatile crowds numbering in the hundreds of thousands have taken place in Paris and elsewhere.

New Zealand (2013)

On April 17, the New Zealand Parliament gave final approval to a measure that legalizes same-sex marriage, making the Pacific island nation the 13th country in the world and the first in the Asia-Pacific region to allow gays and lesbians to wed. The measure won approval by a 77-44 margin in the country's unicameral legislature, including support from Prime

Minister John Key, and was signed by the country's governor-general (a process known as royal assent) on April 19. The law took effect in August 2013.

In 2005, New Zealand enacted legislation allowing same-sex couples to enter into civil unions. The 2013 measure not only legalizes same-sex marriage but also allows for gay and lesbian couples to adopt children.

Uruguay (2013)

On April 10, the lower house of Uruguay's Congress passed legislation legalizing same-sex marriage, a week after the country's Senate did so. President José Mujica signed the bill into law on May 3, making Uruguay the second Latin American country to legalize same-sex marriage, following Argentina. Civil unions have been permitted in Uruguay since 2008, and gay and lesbian couples were given adoption rights in 2009.

In July 2010, Argentina became the first country in Latin America to legalize same-sex marriage.

Uruguay is among the most secular countries in Latin America. A Pew Research Center study on the global religious landscape as of 2010 found that roughly four-in-ten Uruguayans are unaffiliated with a particular religion. About 58 percent of Uruguayans are Christian; in the Latin America-Caribbean region as a whole, 90 percent of the population is Christian.

Denmark (2012)

In June 2012, Denmark's legislature passed a bill legalizing gay marriage. The measure was enacted into law a few days later when Queen Margrethe II gave her royal assent to the bill.

In 1989, Denmark became the first country to allow same-sex couples to register as domestic partners. And in 2010, the country enacted a law allowing gay couples in registered partnerships the right to adopt children.

With the legalization of gay marriage, the Evangelical Lutheran Church in Denmark (which is the state church), is required to allow same-sex couples to marry in churches. However, no member of the church's clergy is required to perform the wedding of a gay or lesbian couple. In addition, the law leaves it up to other religious groups to determine whether or not to allow same-sex weddings in its churches.

Argentina (2010)

In July 2010, Argentina became the first country in Latin America to legalize same-sex marriage. In spite of vigorous opposition from the Catholic Church and evangelical Protestant churches, the measure passed both houses of the Argentine legislature and was signed into law by President Cristina Fernandez de Kirchner. The law grants same-sex couples who marry all the rights and responsibilities enjoyed by heterosexual couples, including the right to adopt children.

In the decade before the enactment of the same-sex marriage law, a number of local jurisdictions, including the nation's capital, Buenos Aires, had enacted laws allowing gays and lesbians to enter into civil unions.

Portugal (2010)

In June 2010, Portugal became the eighth country to legalize same-sex marriage. Its parliament had passed the measure legalizing gay marriage earlier in 2010. But following its passage, Portugal's president, Anibal Cavaco Silva, asked the Constitutional Court to review the measure. In April 2010, the Constitutional Court declared the law to be constitutionally valid. It was signed by Silva in May of that year and took effect one month later. Portugal's gay marriage law does not give married same-sex couples the right to adopt children.

Iceland (2010)

A measure legalizing same-sex marriage passed the Icelandic legislature in June 2010. Public opinion polls prior to the vote indicated broad support for the measure, and no members of the country's legislature voted against it. Iceland had allowed same-sex couples to register as domestic partners since 1996. A decade later, the parliament passed a measure allowing gay couples to adopt children.

After the new law took effect in late June 2010, the country's prime minister, Johanna Sigurdardottir, wed her longtime partner, Jonina Leosdottir, becoming one of the first people to marry under the statute.

Sweden (2009)

In April 2009, the Swedish parliament voted by an overwhelming majority to legalize same-sex marriage. Gay couples in Sweden had been allowed to register for civil unions since 1995.

Since January 2009, gay couples in Norway legally have been able to marry, adopt children and undergo artificial insemination.

The 2009 law allows gays and lesbians to marry in both religious and civil ceremonies, but it does not require clergy to officiate at such ceremonies. The Lutheran-affiliated Church of Sweden, to which roughly three-quarters of all Swedes belong, has offered blessings for same-sex partnerships since January 2007. In October 2009, the church's governing board voted to allow its clergy to officiate at same-sex marriage ceremonies.

Norway (2009)

Since January 2009, gay couples in Norway legally have been able to marry, adopt children and undergo artificial insemination. The new law replaced a 1993 law permitting civil unions. The 2009 law was passed despite resistance from members of the Christian Democratic Party and the Progress Party, as well as a public controversy over state funding for fertility treatments for lesbian couples.

The largest religious group in the country, the Lutheran-affiliated Church of Norway, was split over the issue. Following passage of the new law, the church's leaders voted to prohibit its pastors from conducting same-sex weddings. But the Church of Norway does allow clergy to bless same-sex unions.

South Africa (2006)

The South African parliament legalized same-sex marriage in November 2006, one year after the country's highest court ruled that the previous marriage laws violated the South African constitution's guarantee of equal rights. The new law allows for religious institutions and civil officers to refuse to conduct same-sex marriage ceremonies, a provision that critics claim violates the rights of same-sex couples under the constitution.

The new measure passed by a margin of greater than five-to-one, with support coming from both the governing African National Congress as well as the main opposition party, the Democratic Alliance. However, the traditional monarch of the Zulu people, who account for about one-fifth of the country's population, maintains that homosexuality is morally wrong.

Spain (2005)

A closely divided Spanish parliament legalized same-sex marriage in 2005, guaranteeing identical rights to all married couples regardless of sexual orientation. The new measure added language to the existing marriage statute, which now reads, "Marriage will have the same requirements and results when the two people entering into the contract are of the same sex or of different sexes."

Vatican officials, as well as the Catholic Spanish Bishops Conference, strongly criticized the law, and large crowds demonstrated in Madrid for and against the measure. After the law went into effect, the country's constitutional court rejected challenges from two municipal court judges who had refused marriage licenses to same-sex couples. The high court ruled that the lower court judges lacked legal standing to bring the suits.

Canada (2005)

Same-sex couples in Canada gained most of the legal benefits of marriage in 1999 when the federal and provincial governments extended common law marriages to gay and lesbian couples. Through a series of court cases beginning in 2003, same-sex marriage gradually became legal in nine of the country's 13 provinces and territories. In 2005, the Canadian Parliament passed legislation making same-sex marriage legal nationwide. In 2006, lawmakers defeated an effort by the ruling Conservative Party of Canada to reconsider the issue, leaving the law unchanged.

Support for [Belgium's same-sex marriage] law came from both the Flemish-speaking North and the French-speaking South, and the law generated surprisingly little controversy across the country.

Belgium (2003)

Beginning in 1998, the Belgian parliament offered limited rights to same-sex couples through registered partnerships. Same-sex couples could register with a city clerk and formally assume joint responsibility for a household. Five years later, in January 2003, the Belgian parliament legalized same-sex marriage, giving gay and lesbian couples the same tax and inheritance rights as heterosexual couples.

Support for the law came from both the Flemish-speaking North and the French-speaking South, and the law generated surprisingly little controversy across the country. The long-dominant Christian Democratic Party, traditionally allied with the Catholic Church, was out of power when the parliament passed the measure.

The 2003 law allowed the marriages of Belgian same-sex couples and recognized as married those from other countries where same-sex marriage was legal. Those provisions were broadened in 2004 to allow any same-sex couple to marry as long as one member of the couple had lived in Belgium for at least three months. In 2006, the parliament also granted same-sex partners the right to adopt children.

The Netherlands (2000)

In December 2000, the Netherlands became the first country to legalize same-sex marriage when the Dutch parliament passed, by a three-to-one margin, a landmark bill allowing the practice. The legislation gave same-sex couples the right to marry, divorce and adopt children. The legislation altered a single sentence in the existing civil marriage statute, which now reads, "A marriage can be contracted by two people of different or the same sex."

The only opposition in parliament came from the Christian Democratic Party, which at the time was not part of the governing coalition. After the law went into effect, the Protestant Church in the Netherlands, which then represented about 12% of the country's population, announced that individual congregations could decide whether to conduct same-sex marriage ceremonies. Although Muslim and conservative Christian groups continue to oppose the law, same-sex marriage is widely accepted by the Dutch public.

Countries Where Gay Marriage Is Legal in Some Jurisdictions

Mexico (2009)

In December 2009, the government of Mexico City legalized same-sex marriage within its jurisdiction. The decision was challenged in court, but the law was upheld by Mexico's Supreme Court, which in August 2010 ruled that same-sex marriages performed in Mexico City were valid and that they must be accepted throughout the country. Since 2011, the southern Mexican state of Quintana Roo also has allowed gay marriages.

United States (2003)

Same-sex marriages were first made legal in the U.S. in Massachusetts in 2003, when the state's highest court ruled that the Massachusetts Constitution gives gays and lesbians the right to marry. Now, laws legalizing same-sex marriage are or soon will be in effect in 17 states—California, Connecticut, Delaware, Hawaii, Illinois, Iowa, Maine, Maryland, Massachusetts, Minnesota, New Hampshire, New Jersey, New Mexico, New York, Rhode Island, Vermont and Washington state—and the District of Columbia, with court decisions, legislative action or statewide referendums prompting the changes. In addition, the Supreme Court struck down part of the federal Defense of Marriage Act in 2013, requiring the federal government to recognize same-sex marriages from the states where they are legal.

CHAPTER 2

Does Same-Sex Marriage Benefit Society?

Chapter Preface

It is impossible to overstate the deep and pervasive influence that the institution of marriage has had in shaping human culture over the past few millennia. Although societies have different traditions and models for what exactly constitutes a marriage, as a broad concept marriage is a human universal, an event that is common to all cultures worldwide.

As one of the most basic building blocks of human society, heterosexual marriage provides a framework for human reproduction and child rearing while minimizing group conflict. It also creates deep emotional ties, bonds of social support, and behavioral strictures that help ensure a stable society.

As a global cultural practice, marriage creates formal ties between individuals, families, clans, and often the state; it enforces incest taboos and regulates sexual behavior through social norms; it creates a mechanism for the transfer of child custody as well as wealth, property, and other resources; it bestows and clarifies social status among individuals; and it promotes the communal care and protection of family members, particularly of marital offspring.

"As a deeply rooted social and cultural institution, marriage is powerful in ways that we might not always appreciate and in ways that we certainly cannot control,"[1] writes M.V. Lee Badgett in her book *When Gay People Get Married*, a cross-cultural study of what happens when societies legalize same-sex marriage.

Marriage is not a static tradition, however, and the institution itself is shaped by cultural norms as much as it influences

1. M.V. Lee Badgett, *When Gay People Get Married: What Happens When Societies Legalize Same-Sex Marriage*, New York: New York University Press, 2009.

them. Consequently, the landscape of marriage in much of the modern world has shifted dramatically over time.

Even in the United States, just a few generations ago women and children were still viewed as actual property owned by men, wife beating was perfectly legal, and divorce was prohibited without proof of grievous wrongdoing by a spouse. Interracial marriage was still illegal in some US states until June 1967.

Those things may sound shocking to us today, but those aspects of marriage evolved only because a changing culture demanded it.

In the 1960s and 1970s, as women increasingly delayed marriage and children in favor of careers and education, the powerful movements for civil rights, women's rights, and gay rights converged with the sexual revolution and the introduction of the contraceptive pill to transform the cultural norms around sexual relationships and marriage even further. Consequently, many defenders of traditional marriage believe that these cultural developments have already done irreparable harm to the institution.

Indeed, the numbers show that heterosexual marriage has been falling out of favor in the United States for the past forty years, so much so that now the nationwide percentage of married individuals is the smallest it has ever been.

According to a 2013 report from the National Center for Family and Marriage Research at Bowling Green State University in Ohio, the US marriage rate is currently 31.1, or thirty-one marriages per one thousand unmarried women. In 1920, the national marriage rate was 92.3. Forty-eight percent of new births in the United States in 2013 were to unmarried women, another significant high.

In 2011, a study by the Pew Research Institute found that barely half of Americans over age eighteen were married; the 5 percent drop from the previous year was a sudden decline that stunned researchers.

But while heterosexuals are increasingly turning away from marriage as a part of their long-term relationships and child-rearing protocol, LGBT couples are fighting for the right to participate in an institution from which they have long been excluded.

"Ironically, at a time when many demographers take for granted the 'deinstitutionalization of marriage' for hetero-sexual couples, that is, the fading away of the social and legal meanings of marriage that structure how married people live their lives, the experiences of gay and lesbian couples suggest that marriage has a continuing relevance and meaning,"[2] writes Badgett.

Just what that meaning is and whether the institution of marriage and society itself will change for the better because of it remain to be seen. The authors in this chapter present a variety of arguments for why they believe that sanctioning same-sex marriage is either beneficial or harmful to society.

2. Ibid.

Same-Sex Marriage Benefits Society in Many Ways

Murray Lipp

Murray Lipp is a social justice activist and the administrator of Gay Marriage USA on Facebook.

The legalization of same-sex marriage benefits both LGBT people *and* America as a nation. As two major Supreme Court decisions about same-sex marriage (Proposition 8 and DOMA [Defense of Marriage Act]) loom on the horizon, it's an opportune time to refocus attention on the many advantages associated with the pursuit and achievement of marriage equaility.

There are at least seven ways in which the legalization of gay marriage is beneficial for LGBT Americans and the United States of America.

1. Promotes Equality and Non-Discrimination in Society

Millions of LGBT people contribute daily to American life in a multitude of ways culturally, socially, financially, politically, vocationally, and spiritually. We are fundamental to this nation's continued growth and evolution and the U.S.A. would suffer greatly from the withdrawal of our many contributions. The legalization of same-sex marriage affirms the inherent worthiness of LGBT people as valued American citizens deserving of equal rights under the law.

This promotion of equality and non-discrimination plays an extremely important role in reducing homophobia and in affirming a minority group in society which has for so long endured significant discrimination and stigmatization. Legalizing same-sex marriage communicates to millions of people across the country that gay relationships are of equal value to straight relationships, thereby helping to reduce intergroup prejudice and supporting cultural diversity.

2. Fosters Psychological, Physical, and Social Wellbeing Amongst LGBT People

Same-sex couples are excluded from the institution of marriage in 38 states [at the time this article was written]. Furthermore, the federal government denies legally married same-sex couples more than 1000 federal rights and benefits associated with marriage. This discrimination and institutional exclusion negatively impacts LGBT people in a variety of tangible and practical ways. It can also cause psychological distress, social conflict and ill-health. Equal allocation of marriage rights and benefits to same-sex couples assists LGBT people in a practical sense and the elimination of relationship discrimination helps promote psychosocial and physical wellbeing.

It is to America's benefit when LGBT people are given the freedom to achieve their full potential in life without having to waste precious time and resources battling for basic equality. The act of discrimination is an essentially destructive societal behavior which, ultimately, brings negative consequences both to the oppressors and the oppressed. Ending discrimination in marriage laws goes some way to correcting this.

The denial of equal marriage rights unfairly disadvantages children who are raised by same-sex couples residing in states where gay marriage is not legal or not recognized.

3. Promotes Family Stability and Validates LGBT Family Units

Today's children represent America's future and it is in the country's best interest to support their development, regardless of whom they are parented by. Marriage, as an institution, helps to foster the wellbeing of children by providing married couples with various rights, benefits and protections which can strengthen relationship bonds and family units. Around the nation there are millions of children being raised in households led by same-sex couples, many of whom are denied the right to legally marry in their home state.

Standing Up for Children

The denial of equal marriage rights unfairly disadvantages children who are raised by same-sex couples residing in states where gay marriage is not legal or not recognized. This lack of support for LGBT families denies children within them the same type of protections afforded children in "traditional" families headed by married straight couples. It also sends a damaging message to children within LGBT families that their parents are inferior, second-class citizens who are not worthy of equal treatment in society. The legalization of gay marriage helps to address this injustice by supporting family stability and validating the worthiness of families led by same-sex couples.

4. Provides Economic and Business Opportunities

The legalization of same-sex marriage has consistently been shown to provide an economic boost to those states and countries that have embraced marriage equality. The marriage and wedding industry is a significant one. Allowing gay couples to marry provides businesses in this industry with a large and new market to access. Nearly $260 million was injected into the New York City economy in the year following the legalization of same-sex marriage. Gay marriage tourism benefits those regions which permit same-sex marriage by attracting gay couples from other states and countries where it is not legal.

Most large businesses understand the importance of recognizing gay marriage because it enables them to more readily retain LGBT staff and customers. Not surprisingly, an increasing number of national and global companies are now expressing support for marriage equality and speaking out in favor of gay marriage.

5. Fosters True Freedom of Religion

Freedom of religion allows a person or group to pursue the practice of their religion without governmental interference. It also protects those who do not follow a religion by shielding them from being forced to live in accordance with religious beliefs and values they do not agree with. The legalization of same-sex marriage is consistent with freedom of religion in that it removes from marriage laws religious notions that may have initially shaped those laws.

The Separation of Church and State

There is no hierarchy of religions in a society which truly honors freedom of religion. Accordingly, the religious views of no one particular group should be given preference in the development of marriage laws. While some religions don't support same-sex marriage, others certainly *do* support it. The most fair and ethical approach—which treats all people equally regardless of religious affiliation—is to factor out religious points of view when crafting marriage laws within a secular context.

[The] unfortunate construction of marriage equality as a left vs right and Democratic vs Republican issue wrongly politicizes what is essentially a human rights matter.

---

6. Assists With the De-politicization of LGBT Rights

The politicization of LGBT rights as a left vs right issue has been one of the many "culture wars" that has plagued American society in recent decades. The battle between pro-equality "liberals" and anti-equality "conservatives" continues to characterize the state-by-state legalization of same-sex marriage. Democratic politicians have successfully led legislative efforts to legalize gay marriage in nine states [at the time of this writing]. President Obama's support of marriage equality, Bill Clinton's abandonment of the Defense of Marriage Act (DOMA), and Democratic voters' support of marriage equality contrast strikingly with the situation on the Republican side. Opposition to same-sex marriage remains a key part of the GOP platform and a majority of Republican politicians and GOP voters do not support marriage equality.

This unfortunate construction of marriage equality as a left vs right and Democratic vs Republican issue wrongly politicizes what is essentially a human rights matter. In this sense the legalization of same-sex marriage plays a central role in de-politicizing the quest for LGBT equality. It provides Democrats and Republicans with an opportunity to refocus their efforts on addressing other problems in society and to stop wasting valuable resources on a manufactured culture war.

7. Strengthens National Identity and International Reputation

"Liberty and justice for all" is a phrase often used in descriptions of the U.S.A. which seek to capture the nation's collective psyche, spirit and identity. Historically, America has presented itself as a global leader in matters of freedom and democracy. It's unfortunate and ironic, however, that back on home soil one particular group of people is consistently denied full access to the "American dream." The fact that same-sex marriage is not legal in thirty-eight states of the U.S.A. and not recognized by the federal government has damaged America's international reputation in relation to LGBT rights.

Fifteen countries have moved ahead of the U.S.A. in providing federal marriage equality. The removal of anti-gay discrimination in all state and federal laws that apply to marriage would play a key role in enhancing America's international reputation in matters of social justice and in restoring our integrity as a global leader in the provision of civil and human rights. The tag of "liberty and justice for all" will become more believable when same-sex couples are granted equal access to marriage laws across the country. . . .

Time to Embrace Marriage Equality

It is time to stop playing politics and to stop "debating" whether LGBT Americans should have equal rights in society and whether same-sex relationships should be valued equally under the law. Allowing same-sex couples to marry harms no one. Conversely, it enhances the lives of millions of LGBT Americans and their families and also benefits broader society economically, cuturally, and politically. I look forward to the day when the provision of marriage equality is embraced and valued as a core feature of American culture and when "we the people" can rightly be claimed to include everyone.

Same-Sex Marriage Strengthens the Institution of Marriage

John Gustav-Wrathall

John Gustav-Wrathall is a Minneapolis-based blogger who has been in a committed relationship with his husband for over two decades. He is also a believing Latter-day Saint who has been excommunicated from the Mormon Church because of his homosexuality. He is the author of Why Theology Can't Save Us, and Other Essays on Being Gay and Mormon.

Marriage is about love, family and commitment—*for everyone.* If we look at the specifics of how marriage strengthens and protects loving commitments and provides a more secure framework for home and family, we'll see how and why extending the social recognition and the legal protections of marriage to same-sex couples strengthens everyone's families.

1) Coercing same-sex oriented individuals into mixed orientation marriages is a formula for heart-break and marriage failure. One of the major reasons opponents of same-sex marriage offer for their position is that they believe it is God's will for everyone to be in heterosexual marriages. By denying same-sex couples the social approval that comes with marriage, they assume, opposite-sex marriage will be upheld as the social ideal and more individuals will feel drawn to enter into those kinds of arrangements.

While no one is forcing anyone to marry an opposite-sex spouse against his or her will, this is a subtle form of social coercion/pressure whose end goal is essentially to promote mixed-orientation marriages, the vast majority of which fail. This social policy is, in other words, almost calculated to increase the likelihood of divorce for large numbers of couples.

It is in the best interests of our society to promote *stable, lasting* pair-bondings. Allowing same-sex marriage as an option helps to remove the social stigma on homosexuality. It will encourage same-sex oriented individuals to come out of the closet and pair bond with (marry!) other same-sex oriented individuals. This is what opponents of same-sex marriage do not want. But, it is nevertheless in society's best interests, because it will reduce the likelihood that closeted individuals will enter into inherently unstable unions with persons of the opposite sex. It will correspondingly increase the likelihood that they will form lasting commitments with persons they are attracted to, and who are attracted to them.

Same-sex marriage will decrease divorce and increase family happiness and stability for everyone!

Forcing gay people to be alone weakens the fabric of society.

---

2) We are individually and collectively stronger when we are members of a family. Families are the oldest form of social insurance there is. Being married means you have someone to rely on if you get sick, if you lose your job or if you experience any other form of misfortune. That someone is there to take care of you not just physically, but emotionally and spiritually as well. Often when we experience tragedy, the thing that plays the biggest role in helping us get back on our feet again is the emotional support and encouragement we get from someone who has committed to be our yoke-mate for life. I know this has been true for both me and Göran. In our going on 18 years together, there have been times when one or the other of us has been down and out, and the other has been there as number one cheerleader and supporter.

Marriage Is in Everyone's Best Interest

Opponents of same-sex marriage would prefer that if gay people can't be married to a member of the opposite sex that they be single for life. But in whose best interest is that really? Certainly not in the state's interest. When a person who is alone falls, who is there to help pick him up?

Individuals live in families, families live in societies. If an individual falls, if he has no immediate family, extended family is expected to help. If extended family is non-existent or ineffective, then it falls to the larger society. Forcing gay people to be alone weakens the fabric of society. Because Göran and I have been able to help each other over the years, we are stronger, we've been able to become resources to others. In recent years we have become foster parents, able to provide a loving home to children who have fallen through the cracks of society. So, the fact that we exist as a family unit means *we can provide resources to help care for others*, to become part of the social safety net.

Any one of the personal crises that Göran and I have faced could have proven deadly. That fact that each of us was here for the other increased the likelihood that we are both here today. And we are here today as a family unit that is capable of contributing to our neighborhood, community and state. And so society is stronger.

Same-sex marriage makes all of us stronger.

3) Marriage promotes morality and makes us more spiritually sensitive. Refusing same-sex couples the right to marry essentially sends a message to gay folks that the normal rules and expectations of sexual morality don't apply to us the way they do to everybody else. It also sends another, subtler and more damaging message: that gay people are inferior to heterosexual people. That we don't deserve stability, love or family. That we are inherently morally inferior. This damaging message encourages just the kinds of reckless, immoral behavior that the opponents of same-sex marriage claim to oppose.

By legalizing same-sex marriage, we send gay folks the message that they are expected to abide by the same social norms, the same morality that we expect of everyone else.

The Psychological Impact of Marriage

When Göran and I got married, it had a huge psychological impact on me. I became aware of a profound responsibility to my significant other. It changed the way I thought about myself and about my sexuality. Committing myself to my husband and being willing to bridle my sexuality in a way that honors my love for him and my commitment to him has changed my life in so many ways for the better. In many ways, those commitments paved the way for me to come back to the Church. I believe living in a way that honored my love for him made me more sensitive to the promptings of the Spirit.

It is those spiritual benefits of the kind of love and commitment that can be fostered in marriage that I personally consider one of the greatest benefits of marriage. Though, for obvious reasons—such as social stability and the reduction of sexually transmitted diseases—providing a social framework that discourages promiscuity and encourages sexual morality among gay men and lesbians is also a benefit that strengthens not just the individuals involved, but society as a whole.

Same-Sex Marriage Furthers the American Values of Freedom and Equality

John Corvino

John Corvino is associate professor and chair of philosophy at Wayne State University in Detroit.

A prominent figure in the marriage-equality debate once wrote, "I believe that today the principle of equal dignity must apply to gay and lesbian persons. In that sense, insofar as we are a nation founded on this principle, we would be more American on the day we permitted same-sex marriage than we were the day before." Can you guess who that figure was? Evan Wolfson, the founder and president of Freedom to Marry? Jonathan Rauch? Ted Olson or David Boies, lead attorneys fighting for marriage equality in the California Proposition 8 case? Not even close. It was David Blankenhorn, one of same-sex marriage's strongest opponents.

To his credit, Blankenhorn sees this debate not as a debate of good against evil, but as a debate about competing goods. "One good," he writes, "is the equal dignity of all persons. Another good is a mother and father as every child's birthright." In previous sections, I argued that letting gays marry never deprives a child of its mother or father, and that there are entire "missing staircases" between the premise that children need their own biological parents and the conclusion that we should forbid gays to marry. In this final section, I'll turn to Blankenhorn's positive theme—that marriage equality makes us "more American"—by focusing on the fundamental American values of freedom and equality. I'll begin with freedom.

John Corvino, "The Case for Same-Sex Marriage," in *Debating Same-Sex Marriage*, New York: Oxford University Press, 2012, pp. 83–90. Copyright © 2012 by Oxford University Press. All rights reserved. Reproduced by permission.

My Freedom Versus Yours

One would think that the connection between freedom generally, and the freedom of gays to pursue happiness as they see fit, would be obvious. If only it were so. Just this morning [2012] someone sent me a link to the Texas State Republican Party Platform. In large capital letters on the first page appear the words "*PRESERVING AMERICAN FREEDOM.*" Yet just a few pages later, the same document supports making it a felony for gays to have consensual sex and for any civil official to perform a same-sex wedding service. In other words, these folks are in favor of freedom . . . unless you're going to do things with it that they don't like.

I can appreciate the argument that a liberal society protects religious freedom, and that we should thus allow doctors in non-emergency cases to refer patients to a colleague for procedures that violate their consciences. But what are the limits of such exemptions?

Sadly, this warped sense of freedom is not an anomaly. To the contrary, it is becoming a familiar theme in the fight against marriage equality. Consider the now-infamous "Gathering Storm" ad put out by [Maggie] Gallagher's National Organization for Marriage (NOM). (Google it: it has been immortalized on YouTube, along with dozens of hilarious parodies.) The ad was part of NOM's 2009 "religious-liberty campaign" following marriage-equality victories in Vermont and Iowa. In it, various characters warn that their fundamental liberties are under threat:

> There's a storm gathering. The clouds are dark, and the winds are strong, and I am afraid. Some who advocate for same-sex marriage have taken the issue far beyond same-sex couples. They want to bring the issue into my life. My freedom will be taken away. . . . [S]ome who advocate same-sex

marriage have not been content with same-sex couples living as they wish. Those advocates want to change the way I live. I will have no choice. . . .

If you didn't know better, you would think that some states had just made same-sex marriage mandatory for everyone. But of course they didn't. Heterosexual marriage is, and will remain, an option in all fifty states. Marriage licenses are not a finite resource, where giving them to gays means taking them away from straights. There is, in Evan Wolfson's apt phrase, "enough marriage to share."

Dissecting the NOM Ad

How does marriage for gays take liberty away from heterosexuals? The ad mentions three cases—presumably the most compelling available examples at the time—to illustrate the alleged danger:

> *"I'm a California doctor who must choose between my faith and my job."*

Not exactly. The case in question involved a doctor who declined to perform artificial insemination for an (unmarried) lesbian, thus violating California antidiscrimination law. I can appreciate the argument that a liberal society protects religious freedom, and that we should thus allow doctors in nonemergency cases to refer patients to a colleague for procedures that violate their consciences. But what are the limits of such exemptions? What if a doctor opposed divorce, and thus refused to perform insemination for a heterosexual woman in her second marriage? What if she opposed interfaith marriage, and refused to perform insemination for a Christian married to a Jew, or even for a Catholic married to a Methodist? Or what if a doctor refused to perform insemination for anyone except Muslims, on the grounds that children ought only to be raised in Muslim households? These are questions that marriage-equality opponents never bother to consider when playing the religious-liberty card. I'm not saying that the answers are obvious, but the tension between professional responsibility and personal religious conviction is hardly unique to the gay case.

The main problem, however, is that this case is a red herring. The real objection here is not to marriage, but to antidiscrimination laws, which pre-dated marriage equality in California. California law prohibits healthcare providers from discriminating on the basis of both sexual orientation and marital status, among other factors. Whether this doctor's patient was married (or could or should be married) was not at issue. (In fact, at the time of the incident, marriage was not available for same-sex couples in California.)

What these complaints make clear is that by "freedom," marriage-equality opponents mean the freedom to live in a world where they never have to confront the fact that others choose to exercise their freedom differently.

Antidiscrimination Laws

Gallagher makes the same mistake later in this book, when she discusses the "most egregious case" of Illinois, which no longer grants to Catholic Charities state contracts for adoption services. As the *State Journal-Register* explained, in a passage quoted by Gallagher herself, "This case had less to do with any religious organizations acceptance or recognition of civil unions than it did with reinforcing the antidiscrimination element of the law that created civil unions in Illinois." In other words, it was the fact that Illinois prohibits discrimination on the basis of sexual orientation, not its stance on marriage or civil unions, that created the conflict for Catholic Charities. Antidiscrimination law and marriage law are not the same thing.

"I'm part of a New Jersey church group punished by the government because we can't support same-sex marriage."

No, you're (an actor playing) part of a New Jersey church group that operates Ocean Grove Camp. Ocean Grove Camp received a property-tax exemption by promising to make its grounds open to the public; it also received substantial tax dollars to support the facility's maintenance. It then chose to exclude some of those taxpayers—in this case, a lesbian couple wishing to use the camp's allegedly "public" pavilion for their civil-union ceremony. So New Jersey did the right thing and revoked the pavilion's (though not the whole camp's) property-tax exemption. Once again, the issue here is not marriage—which New Jersey did not and still does not have for same-sex couples—it's nondiscrimination law related to public accommodations.

"I am a Massachusetts parent helplessly watching public schools teach my son that gay marriage is OK."

Sort of. As long as marriage is legal for same-sex couples in Massachusetts, public schools will naturally teach that it's legal. That's part of educating students about the world around them. But at home Massachusetts parents can add whatever evaluative judgments they'd like, on this or any issue. What they cannot do is censor public-school curriculum so that it mentions only the families they like. After all, Massachusetts parents—like all states' parents and taxpayers—include same-sex households.

What these complaints make clear is that by "freedom," marriage-equality opponents mean the freedom to live in a world where they never have to confront the fact that others choose to exercise their freedom differently. In other words, they intend the very opposite of a free society.

The grain of truth in the NOM ad is this: marriage is a public institution. That means that everyone is required to respect the legal boundaries of marriages that they might not condone. But that has always been true. My mother-in-law believes that "real" marriages must originate in a Catholic church, preferably in the context of a nuptial mass. She was horrified when her daughter chose to marry on a beach at a tropical resort with a justice of the peace officiating. But her daughter did so, and the law now requires my mother-in-law—and everyone else—to treat the couple as legally married. Now imagine that my mother-in-law demanded that the law prohibit such marriages on the grounds that they interfere with her freedom. This is exactly what Gallagher and NOM are doing when they argue that same-sex marriage restricts their religious liberty. Religious liberty does not include the liberty to live in a world where the law enforces your particular religion's conception of marriage. Just the opposite.

Once the state provides marriage as an option for different-sex partners . . . but then denies it to same-sex couples, it is treating citizens unequally.

Selective Interpretation

Notice, too, how those who cite religion to justify their opposition to legal same-sex marriage are remarkably selective. The Christian Bible forcefully condemns divorce, with Jesus himself repeating the Genesis teaching that no one may separate what God has joined, and adding that those who divorce are tantamount to adulterers. (Note also that the common secular rationale for opposing marriage equality—that children need mothers and fathers—seems far more relevant to divorce.) Yet there is no significant movement, religious or otherwise, for banning divorce. In other words, marriage-equality opponents are quite willing to subject the gay and lesbian minority to a far more restrictive standard than they would ever tolerate for themselves.

At the beginning of this book, I wrote that the marriage-equality debate affects "everyone who has a stake in what family means." That is true. But it does not affect everyone equally. When marriage-equality opponents complain about gay-rights advocates "changing the definition of marriage for everyone," their wording misleads. No one is trying to take heterosexual marriage away from straight people. Whatever happens in this debate, Maggie Gallagher and other heterosexuals will retain the full legal right to marry the partners of their choosing. The question is whether they will have that right in a world where their gay and lesbian fellow citizens enjoy the same right. The question is one of equal treatment under the law.

Marriage-equality opponents sometimes retort that gay and lesbian citizens already enjoy the equal right to marry, because they, like everyone else, can marry someone of the opposite sex. But this response is specious. Formally speaking, it has the same structure as a long-discredited argument supporting antimiscegenation laws: whites can marry within their race; nonwhites can marry within their race; therefore everyone has equal marriage rights. The problem with this antimiscegenation argument is not merely that the white/nonwhite distinction is arbitrary—which it is, in the same way that the male/female distinction is arbitrary for virtually all of marriage's purposes besides biological procreation. The problem is that the argument treats "equality" as a purely formal notion, rather than a substantive one. As long as gay and lesbian *couples* lack the right to marry, gay and lesbian individuals do not enjoy the right to marry in any substantive sense.

"Enough Marriage to Share"

This point is relevant for those making a Constitutional argument for marriage equality, something I do not intend to do here, beyond these brief closing words. The Fourteenth Amendment of the U.S. Constitution guarantees the "equal protection of the laws." By itself, I don't believe that this guarantee automatically gives anyone—gay or straight—the right to marry, at least not in the sense of a particular kind of state recognition. As [ethicist] Martha Nussbaum (among others) has argued, there are various ways in which the state might consistently and fairly treat its citizens, including getting out of the marriage business altogether. But once the state provides marriage as an option for different-sex partners, even if they cannot or choose not to have children; even if they are elderly; even if they are divorced; even if they are incapable of coitus, and thus what the new-natural-law theorists consider "real marriage"—once the state provides marriage in all these diverse cases and more, but then denies it to same-sex couples, it is treating citizens unequally.

We can do better. As a just society, premised on ideals of freedom and equality, we ought to do better. There is enough marriage to share.

Marriage Equality Reduces Dependence on Government Social Services

Josh Barro

Josh Barro is the lead writer for The Ticker, *a blog on Bloomberg.com that focuses on economics, politics, policy, and global affairs.*

A lot of people have the same question for the gay fiscal-policy writer: How would same-sex marriage affect government budgets? There's been a surprisingly large amount of research into this question, and the answer is that same-sex marriage would probably improve governments' fiscal situations a little.

The Congressional Budget Office looked into the question in 2004 at the request of Republican Representative Steve Chabot of Ohio. The CBO's findings suggest that federally recognized gay marriage would reduce the budget deficit by about $450 million a year, or roughly 0.01 percent of total federal spending. So, I'm sorry, straight America: We're not going to balance your budget by getting married, but we'll help a little bit.

The more interesting part is how same-sex marriage affects the budget. Most people will think of it as changing income taxes and benefits for gay public employees. But some of the biggest effects come in welfare programs: Marriage makes people more robust against financial shocks and less likely to qualify for welfare programs. Same-sex marriage would save hundreds of millions of dollars a year by getting some gay men and lesbians off the Medicaid and Supplemental Security Income rolls.

Revenues and Expenses

On the revenue side, the CBO estimated that gay marriage in all 50 states would increase tax receipts by about $400 million a year if the George W. Bush tax cuts were extended and by about $700 million a year if they were not. Because those tax cuts ended up being mostly extended, the answer is probably somewhere in the middle, but closer to $400 million.

The added revenue comes from the "marriage penalty": Two-earner married couples where each spouse has a similar income tend to be taxed more heavily than they would be if both partners were single. Other couples get a "marriage bonus," generally when the spouses' incomes are very unequal, but the marriage penalty effect is more important.

On the expense side, gay men and lesbians would get access to Social Security benefits based on spousal income. This would raise benefits for some couples, particularly those in which one spouse had much higher career earnings than the other. The CBO estimated these added benefits would cost $350 million a year by 2014.

Gay marriage has a small but positive fiscal effect [on the US budget].

The other main area of added expense would be benefits for the same-sex spouses of federal employees and retirees. The CBO estimated that covering same-sex spouses in the Federal Employee Health Benefits Program would cost about $80 million a year.

But there would be savings in means-tested entitlement programs, as fewer gay men and lesbians would qualify. The CBO estimated annual savings in 2014 of $100 million in

Supplemental Security Income, $300 million in Medicaid and $50 million in Medicare. That makes for a wash on the expense side: $430 million in added costs and $450 million in reduced costs.

The CBO letter is an incomplete look at the federal budget. It doesn't examine the cost of benefits to the same-sex spouses of military service members, which would probably be at least as large as the cost of benefits for civilian employees. On the other hand, the letter predates the Patient Protection and Affordable Care Act [health-care reform bill], which creates another means-tested entitlement whose costs would be reduced by same-sex marriage. A more thorough analysis would probably lead to the same finding: Gay marriage has a small but positive fiscal effect.

States Would Feel Effect Too

States would also face fiscal effects from gay marriage, and their concerns are somewhat different from the federal government's. States spend a much larger percentage of their budgets on employee compensation than the federal government does, so the cost of benefits for employees' same-sex spouses is relatively important. On the other hand, states bear no part of the cost of Social Security and do spend a lot on means-tested entitlements.

Even though the cost components are different, the net effect would probably be similar at the state and federal levels: positive, but very small. The Williams Institute at UCLA [University of California Los Angeles] School of Law has reached this conclusion in fiscal analyses across various states; for example, they estimated in 2009 that legal same-sex marriage in Maine would generate $8 million in annual fiscal benefits for the state, mostly through reductions in Medicaid and other public assistance payments.

The fiscal benefits aren't a crucial reason to support same-sex marriage, but they do lend support to one of the "conservative" cases for it. Marriage is a structure through which people depend on each other, so they don't have to depend on the government. For gay men and lesbians to take advantage of that fiscally friendly option, the government has to make it legal for us to marry.

What's Wrong with Letting Same-Sex Couples "Marry?"

Peter Sprigg

Peter Sprigg is a senior fellow for policy studies at the Family Research Council, a conservative Christian group that opposes same-sex marriage and promotes traditional family values.

What's wrong with letting same-sex couples legally "Marry?"

There are two key reasons why the legal rights, benefits, and responsibilities of civil marriage should not be extended to same-sex couples.

The first is that homosexual relationships are not marriage. That is, they simply do not fit the minimum necessary condition for a marriage to exist—namely, the union of a man and a woman.

The second is that homosexual relationships are harmful. Not only do they not provide the same benefits to society as heterosexual marriages, but their consequences are far more negative than positive.

Either argument, standing alone, is sufficient to reject the claim that same-sex unions should be granted the legal status of marriage.

Let's look at the first argument. Isn't marriage whatever the law says it is?

No. Marriage is not a creation of the law. Marriage is a fundamental human institution that predates the law and the Constitution. At its heart, it is an anthropological and sociological reality, not a legal one. Laws relating to marriage merely recognize and regulate an institution that already exists.

But isn't marriage just a way of recognizing people who love each other and want to spend their lives together?

If love and companionship were sufficient to define marriage, then there would be no reason to deny "marriage" to unions of a child and an adult, or an adult child and his or her aging parent, or to roommates who have no sexual relationship, or to groups rather than couples. Love and companionship are usually considered integral to marriage in our culture, but they are not sufficient to define it as an institution.

We still recognize childless marriages because it would be an invasion of a heterosexual couple's privacy to require that they prove their intent or ability to bear children.

All right—but if you add a sexual relationship to love and companionship, isn't that what most people would consider "marriage?"

It's getting closer but is still not sufficient to define marriage.

In a ruling handed down June 26, 2003, the U.S. Supreme Court declared in *Lawrence v. Texas* that sodomy laws (and any other laws restricting private sexual conduct between consenting adults) are unconstitutional. Some observers have suggested that this decision paves the way for same-sex "marriage." But in an ironic way, the Court's rulings that sex need not be (legally) confined to marriage undermine any argument that sex alone is a defining characteristic of marriage. Something more must be required.

So—what IS marriage, then?

Anthropologist Kingsley Davis has said, "The unique trait of what is commonly called marriage is social recognition and approval . . . of a couple's engaging in sexual intercourse and bearing and rearing children." Marriage scholar Maggie Gallagher says that "marriage across societies is a public sexual union that creates kinship obligations and sharing of resources between men, women, and the children their sexual union may produce."

Canadian scholar Margaret A. Somerville says, "Through marriage our society marks out the relationship of two people who will together transmit human life to the next generation and nurture and protect that life."

Another Canadian scholar, Paul Nathanson (who is himself a homosexual), has said, "Because heterosexuality is directly related to both reproduction and survival, . . . *every* human societ[y] has had to *promote* it actively. . . . Heterosexuality is always *fostered* by a cultural norm" that limits marriage to unions of men and women. He adds that people "are wrong in assuming that any society can do without it." [emphasis in original]

Are you saying that married couples who don't have children (whether by choice, or because of infertility or age) aren't really married? If we deny marriage to same-sex couples because they can't reproduce, why not deny it to those couples, too?

A couple that doesn't want children when they marry *might* change their minds. Birth control might fail for a couple that uses it. A couple that appears to be infertile may get a surprise and conceive a child. The marital commitment may deter an older man from conceiving children with a younger woman outside of marriage. Even a very elderly couple is of the structural type (i.e., a man and a woman) that could theoretically produce children (or could have in the past). And the sexual union of all such couples is of the same *type* as that which reproduces the human race, even if it does not have that effect in particular cases.

Admittedly, society's interest in marriages that do not produce children is less than its interest in marriages that result in the reproduction of the species. However, we still recognize childless marriages because it would be an invasion of a heterosexual couple's privacy to require that they prove their intent or ability to bear children.

There is no reason, though, to extend "marriage" to same-sex couples, which are of a structural type (two men or two women) that is incapable—ever, under any circumstances, regardless of age, health, or intent—of producing babies naturally. In fact, they are incapable of even engaging in the type of sexual act that results in natural reproduction. And it takes no invasion of privacy or drawing of arbitrary upper age boundaries to determine that.

Another way to view the relationship of marriage to reproduction is to turn the question around. Instead of asking whether actual reproduction is essential to marriage, ask this: If marriage *never* had *anything* to do with reproduction, would there be any reason for the government to be involved in regulating or rewarding it? Would we even *tolerate* the government intervening in such an intimate relationship, any more than if government defined the terms of who may be your "best friend?" The answer is undoubtedly "no"—which reinforces the conclusion that reproduction is a central (even if not obligatory) part of the social significance of marriage.

Indeed, the facts that a child cannot reproduce, that close relatives cannot reproduce without risk, and that it only takes one man and one woman to reproduce, are among the reasons why people are barred from marrying a child, a close blood relative, or a person who is already married. Concerns about reproduction are central to those restrictions on one's choice of marriage partner—just as they are central to the restriction against "marrying" a person of the same sex.

But people can also reproduce without getting married. So what is the purpose of marriage?

The mere biological conception and birth of children are not sufficient to ensure the reproduction of a healthy, successful society. Paul Nathanson, the homosexual scholar cited above, says that there are at least five functions that marriage serves—things that every culture *must* do in order to survive and thrive. They are:

- Foster the bonding between men and women
- Foster the birth and rearing of children
- Foster the bonding between men and children
- Foster some form of healthy masculine identity
- Foster the transformation of adolescents into sexually responsible adults

Maggie Gallagher puts it more simply, saying that "children need mothers and fathers" and "marriage is the most practical way to get them for children."

Every person, whether heterosexual or homosexual, is subject to legal restrictions as to whom they may marry.

But why should homosexuals be denied the right to marry like anyone else?

The fundamental "right to marry" is a right that rests with *individuals*, not with *couples*. Homosexual *individuals* already have exactly the same "right" to marry as anyone else. Marriage license applications do not inquire as to a person's "sexual orientation."

Many people who now identify themselves as homosexual have previously been in legal (opposite-sex) marriages. On the other hand, many people who previously had homosexual relationships have now renounced that behavior and married persons of the opposite sex. If we define a "homosexual" as anyone who has ever experienced homosexual attractions, then both of these scenarios represent "homosexual" individuals who have exercised their right to be legally married.

However, while every individual person is free to get married, *no* person, whether heterosexual or homosexual, has ever had a legal right to marry simply any willing partner. Every person, whether heterosexual or homosexual, is subject to legal restrictions as to whom they may marry. To be specific, every person, regardless of sexual preference, is legally barred from marrying a child, a close blood relative, a person who is already married, or [in thirty-three states] a person of the same sex. There is no discrimination here, nor does such a policy deny anyone the "equal protection of the laws" (as guaranteed by the Constitution), since these restrictions apply equally to every individual.

Some people may wish to do away with one or more of these longstanding restrictions upon one's choice of marital partner. However, the fact that a tiny but vocal minority of Americans desire to have someone of the same sex as a partner does not mean that they have a "right" to do so, any more than the desires of other tiny (but less vocal) minorities of Americans give them a "right" to choose a child, their own brother or sister, or a group of two or more as their marital partners.

It's true that American society's concept of marriage has changed, especially over the last fifty years. But not all change is positive.

Isn't prohibiting homosexual "marriage" just as discriminatory as prohibiting interracial marriage, like some states used to do?

This analogy is not valid at all. Bridging the divide of the sexes by uniting men and women is both a worthy goal and a part of the fundamental purpose of marriage, common to all human civilizations.

Laws against interracial marriage, on the other hand, served only the purpose of preserving a social system of racial segregation. This was both an unworthy goal and one utterly irrelevant to the fundamental nature of marriage.

Allowing a black woman to marry a white man does not change the definition of marriage, which requires one man and one woman. Allowing two men or two women to marry would change that fundamental definition. Banning the "marriage" of same-sex couples is therefore essential to preserve the nature and purpose of marriage itself.

Hasn't the nature of marriage already changed dramatically in the last few generations? In defending "traditional marriage," aren't you defending something that no longer exists?

It's true that American society's concept of marriage has changed, especially over the last fifty years. But not all change is positive, and our experiences in that regard may be instructive. Consider some of the recent changes to the institution of marriage—and their consequences:

The divorce revolution has undermined the concept that marriage is a life-long commitment. As a result, there's been an epidemic of broken homes and broken families, and the consequences have been overwhelmingly negative.

The sexual revolution has undermined the concept that sexual relations should be confined to marriage. As a result, there's been an epidemic of cohabitation, sexually transmitted diseases, abortions, and broken hearts, and the consequences have been overwhelmingly negative.

The concept that childbearing should be confined to marriage has been undermined. As a result, there's been an epidemic of out-of-wedlock births, single parenthood, and fatherless children, and the consequences have been overwhelmingly negative.

The pornography revolution, particularly with the advent of the Internet, has undermined the concept that a man's sexual desires should be directed toward his wife. As a result, there's been an epidemic of broken relationships, abused wives, and sex crimes, and the consequences have been overwhelmingly negative.

And now there is social and political pressure to redefine what constitutes marriage itself. What grounds does anyone have for thinking that the consequences of that radical social revolution, unprecedented in human history, would be any more positive than the consequences of the much less sweeping changes already described?

Why does "defending marriage" and "defending the family" require opposing same-sex unions? How does a homosexual union do any harm to someone else's heterosexual marriage?

It may come as a surprise to many people, but homosexual unions often have a more direct impact on heterosexual marriages than one would think. For example, the *Boston Globe* reported June 29, 2003, that "nearly 40 percent" of the 5,700 homosexual couples who have entered into "civil unions" in Vermont "have had a previous heterosexual marriage."

Expanding the definition of what "marriage" is to include relationships of a homosexual nature would inevitably, in the long run, change people's concept of what marriage is, what it requires, and what one should expect from it.

Of course, it could be argued that many of those marriages may have ended long before a spouse found their current homosexual partner. And some may assume that no opposite-sex spouse would *want* to remain married to someone with same-sex attractions. Nevertheless, the popular myth that a homosexual orientation is fixed at birth and unchangeable may have blinded us to the fact that many supposed "homosexuals" have, in fact, had perfectly functional heterosexual marriages. And as *Globe* columnist Jeff Jacoby points out, "In another time or another state, some of those marriages might have worked out. The old stigmas, the universal standards that were so important to family stability, might have given them a fighting chance. Without them, they were left exposed and vulnerable."

But isn't the number of homosexuals too small for same-sex unions to have much impact on other people's marriages?

It's probably true that the percentage of marriages that fail because of the desire of one spouse to pursue a homosexual relationship will always be fairly small.

Some have argued that marriage will change the behavior of homosexuals, but it is far more plausible that the behavior of homosexuals will change people's idea of marriage.

The most significant impact of legally recognizing same-sex unions would be more indirect. Expanding the definition of what "marriage" is to include relationships of a homosexual nature would inevitably, in the long run, change people's concept of what marriage is, what it requires, and what one should expect from it. These changes in the popular understanding of marriage would, in turn, change people's behavior both before and during marriage.

How would allowing same-sex couples to marry change society's concept of marriage?

For one thing, it would reinforce many of the negative changes described above. As an example, marriage will open wide the door to homosexual adoption, which will simply lead to more children suffering the negative consequences of growing up without both a mother and a father.

Among homosexual men in particular, casual sex, rather than committed relationships, is the rule and not the exception. And even when they do enter into a more committed relationship, it is usually of relatively short duration. For example, a study of homosexual men in the Netherlands (the first country in the world to legalize "marriage" for same-sex couples), published in the journal *AIDS* in 2003, found that the average length of "steady partnerships" was not more than 2 < years.

In addition, studies have shown that even homosexual men who are in "committed" relationships are not sexually faithful to each other. While infidelity among heterosexuals is much too common, it does not begin to compare to the rates among homosexual men. The 1994 National Health and Social Life Survey, which remains the most comprehensive study of Americans' sexual practices ever undertaken, found that 75 percent of married men and 90 percent of married women had been sexually faithful to their spouse. On the other hand, a major study of homosexual men in "committed" relationships found that only seven out of 156 had been sexually faithful, or 4.5 percent. The Dutch study cited above found that even homosexual men in "steady partnerships" had an average of eight "casual" sex partners per year.

So if same-sex relationships are legally recognized as "marriage," the idea of marriage as a sexually exclusive and faithful relationship will be dealt a serious blow. Adding monogamy and faithfulness to the other pillars of marriage that have already fallen will have overwhelmingly negative consequences for Americans' physical and mental health.

If you want people to be faithful and monogamous, shouldn't you grant same-sex couples the right to marry in order to encourage that?

Some have argued that marriage will change the behavior of homosexuals, but it is far more plausible that the behavior of homosexuals will change people's idea of marriage, further undermining the concepts that marriage is a lifelong commitment and that sex should be confined to marriage.

The entire "gay liberation" movement has been but a part of the larger sexual liberation movement whose fundamental tenet is that anybody should be able to have sex with anybody they want any time they want. To suggest that the crowning achievement of that pro-homosexual movement—obtaining society's ultimate stamp of approval through civil marriage—is suddenly going to result in these "liberated" homosexuals settling down into faithful, monogamous, childrearing is foolishly naive.

Don't homosexuals need marriage rights so that they will be able to visit their partners in the hospital?

The idea that homosexuals are routinely denied the right to visit their partners in the hospital is nonsense. When this issue was raised during debate over the Defense of Marriage Act in 1996, the Family Research Council did an informal survey of nine hospitals in four states and the District of Columbia. None of the administrators surveyed could recall a single case in which a visitor was barred because of their homosexuality, and they were incredulous that this would even be considered an issue.

Except when a doctor limits visitation for medical reasons, final authority over who may visit an adult patient rests with that patient. This is and should be the case regardless of the sexual orientation or marital status of the patient or the visitor.

The only situation in which there would be a possibility that the blood relatives of a patient might attempt to exclude the patient's homosexual partner is if the patient is unable to express his or her wishes due to unconsciousness or mental incapacity. Homosexual partners concerned about this (remote) possibility can effectively preclude it by granting to one another a health care proxy (the legal right to make medical decisions for the patient) and a power of attorney (the right to make all legal decisions for another person). Marriage is not necessary for this. It is inconceivable that a hospital would exclude someone who holds the health care proxy and power of attorney for a patient from visiting that patient, except for medical reasons.

The hypothetical "hospital visitation hardship" is nothing but an emotional smokescreen to distract people from the more serious implications of radically redefining marriage.

Don't homosexuals need the right to marry each other in order to ensure that they will be able to leave their estates to their partner when they die?

As with the hospital visitation issue, the concern over inheritance rights is something that simply does not require marriage to resolve it. Nothing in current law prevents homosexual partners from being joint owners of property such as a home or a car, in which case the survivor would automatically become the owner if the partner dies.

An individual may leave the remainder of his estate to whomever he wishes—again, without regard to sexual orientation or marital status—simply by writing a will. As with the hospital visitation issue, blood relatives would only be able to overrule the surviving homosexual partner in the event that the deceased had failed to record his wishes in a common, inexpensive legal document. Changing the definition of a fundamental social institution like marriage is a rather extreme way of addressing this issue. Preparing a will is a much simpler solution.

Don't homosexuals need marriage rights so that they can get Social Security survivor benefits when a partner dies?

It is ironic that activists are now seeking Social Security survivor benefits for homosexual partners, since Congress originally intended them as a way of supporting a very traditional family structure—one in which the husband worked to provide the family's cash income while the wife stayed home to keep house and raise the children. Social Security survivor benefits were designed to recognize the non-monetary contribution made to a family by the homemaking and child-rearing activities of a wife and mother, and to ensure that a woman and her children would not become destitute if the husband and father were to die.

The Supreme Court ruled in the 1970s that such benefits must be gender-neutral. However, they still are largely based on the premise of a division of roles within a couple between a breadwinner who works to raise money and a homemaker who stays home to raise children.

Very few homosexual couples organize their lives along the lines of such a "traditional" division of labor and roles. They are far more likely to consist of two earners, each of whom can be supported in old age by their own personal Social Security pension.

Furthermore, far fewer homosexual couples than heterosexual ones are raising children at all, for the obvious reason that they are incapable of natural reproduction with each other. This, too, reduces the likelihood of a traditional division of labor among them.

Survivor benefits for the legal (biological or adopted) children of homosexual parents (as opposed to their partners) are already available under current law, so "marriage" rights for homosexual couples are unnecessary to protect the interests of these children themselves.

Don't some scholars claim that some cultures have recognized same-sex unions?

A few pro-homosexual writers, such as William N. Eskridge, Jr. (author of a 1996 book called *The Case for Same-Sex Marriage*), have asserted this. They support this claim by citing evidence, mostly from obscure, primitive tribes, suggesting some tolerance of gender non-conformity or even homosexual relationships (particularly between men and boys). But the important point is that in none of these cultures was such behavior seen as the moral and social equivalent of lifelong heterosexual marriage, which is what today's pro-homosexual activists are demanding.

Even if "marriage" itself is uniquely heterosexual, doesn't fairness require that the legal and financial benefits of marriage be granted to same-sex couples—perhaps through "civil unions" or "domestic partnerships?"

No. The legal and financial benefits of marriage are not an entitlement to be distributed equally to all (if they were, single people would have as much reason to consider them "discriminatory" as same-sex couples). Society grants benefits to marriage because marriage has benefits for society—including, but not limited to, the reproduction of the species in households with the optimal household structure (i.e., the presence of both a mother and a father).

Homosexual relationships, on the other hand, have no comparable benefit for society, and in fact impose substantial costs on society. The fact that AIDS is at least ten times more common among men who have sex with men than among the general population is but one example.

How else does marriage benefit society?

As a group of thirteen leading social scientists reported in 2002, "Marriage is an important social good, associated with an impressively broad array of positive outcomes for children and adults alike." Put simply, married men and women, and their children, are happier, healthier, and more prosperous than people in other types of households.

For example:

- A five-year study released in 1998 found that continuously married husbands and wives experience better emotional health and less depression than people of any other marital status.

- A 1990 review of research found that husbands and wives also have better physical health, while the unmarried have significantly higher annual death rates—about 50 percent higher for women and 250 percent higher for men.

- Rates of violent abuse by intimate partners are four times higher among never-married women, and twelve times higher among divorced and separated women, than they are among married women. In fact, married people are less likely to be the victims of any type of violent crime than are those who have divorced, separated, or never married.

- Families headed by married couples also have much higher incomes and greater financial assets.

- In addition, husbands and wives who are sexually faithful even experience more physical pleasure and emotional satisfaction in their sexual relations than do any other sexually active people.

Children raised by their married mother and father, meanwhile, experience lower rates of many social problems, including: premarital childbearing; illicit drug use; arrest; health, emotional, or behavioral problems; poverty; and school failure or expulsion.

These benefits are then passed on to future generations as well, because children raised by married parents are themselves less likely to cohabit or to divorce as adults.

Isn't it possible that allowing homosexuals to "marry" each other would allow them to participate in those benefits as well?

No. The benefits of marriage do not flow simply from the presence of two people and government recognition of their relationship. Instead, they flow from the inherent complementarity of the sexes and the power of lifelong commitment. The first of these is rejected outright by homosexuals, and the second is far less common among them.

As noted earlier, opening the gates of "marriage" to homosexuals is far more likely to change the attitudes and behavior of heterosexuals for the worse than it is to change the lifestyles of homosexuals for the better.

Do most same-sex couples even want to assume the responsibilities of marriage?

There is considerable reason to doubt that they do. A front-page article in the *New York Times* (August 31, 2003) reported that in the first two months after Ontario's highest court legalized "marriage" for same-sex couples, fewer than 500 same-sex Canadian couples had taken out marriage licenses in Toronto, even though the city has over 6,000 such couples registered as permanent partners.

The *Times* reported that "skepticism about marriage is a recurring refrain among Canadian gay couples," noting that "many gays express the fear that it will undermine their notions of who they are. They say they want to maintain the unique aspects of their culture and their place at the edge of social change." Mitchel Raphael, the editor of a Toronto "gay" magazine, said, "I'd be for marriage if I thought gay people would challenge and change the institution and not buy into the traditional meaning of 'till death do us part' and monogamy forever." And Rinaldo Walcott, a sociologist at the University of Tornoto, lamented, "Will queers now have to live with the heterosexual forms of guilt associated with something called cheating?"

It appears that many homosexuals want the right to "marry" only because marriage constitutes society's ultimate stamp of approval on a sexual relationship—not because they actually want to participate in the institution of marriage as it has historically been understood.

What about the argument that homosexual relations are harmful? What do you mean by that?

Homosexual men experience higher rates of many diseases, including: Human Papillomavirus (HPV), which causes most cases of cervical cancer in women and anal cancer in men; Hepatitis A, B, and C; Gonorrhea; Syphilis; "Gay Bowel Syndrome," a set of sexually transmitted gastrointestinal problems such as proctitis, proctocolitis, and enteritis; HIV/AIDS (One Canadian study found that as a result of HIV alone, "life expectancy for gay and bisexual men is eight to twenty years less than for all men.")

Lesbian women, meanwhile, have a higher prevalence of: Bacterial vaginosis; Hepatitis C; HIV risk behaviors; Cancer risk factors such as smoking, alcohol use, poor diet, and being overweight.

Why do homosexuals have such high rates of sexually transmitted diseases?

Much of the reason for high rates of sexually transmitted diseases among homosexuals lies in their higher rates of promiscuous sexual behavior. For example, the 2003 Dutch study mentioned earlier found that even homosexual men who had a "steady partner" also had an average of eight "casual" sexual partners per year (those without a "steady partner" had an average of 22 "casual" ones). Lesbians, meanwhile, were found by one study to have twice as many lifetime male sexual partners as women in the heterosexual control group.

Do homosexuals have more mental health problems as well?

Yes. Various research studies have found that homosexuals have higher rates of: Alcohol abuse; Drug abuse; Nicotine dependence; Depression; Suicide.

Isn't it possible that these problems result from society's "discrimination" against homosexuals?

This is the argument usually put forward by pro-homosexual activists. However, there is a simple way to test this hypothesis. If "discrimination" were the cause of homosexuals' mental health problems, then one would expect those problems to be much less common in cities or countries, like San Francisco or the Netherlands, where homosexuality has achieved the highest levels of acceptance.

In fact, the opposite is the case. In places where homosexuality is widely accepted, the physical and mental health problems of homosexuals are greater, not less. This suggests that the real problem lies in the homosexual lifestyle itself, not in society's response to it. In fact, it suggests that increasing the level of social support for homosexual behavior (by, for instance, allowing same-sex couple to "marry") would only increase these problems, not reduce them.

Do homosexuals have higher rates of domestic violence?

Yes. It's notable that so-called "hate crimes" directed at homosexuals, such as the brutal murder of Wyoming college student Matthew Shepard in 1998, are often touted as a measure of society's supposed hostility to homosexuals. Yet even when it comes to violence, homosexuals are far more likely to be victimized by each other than by an "anti-gay" attacker. Government statistics show that "intimate partner violence" between people of the same sex is approximately twenty times more common than anti-homosexual "hate crimes."

Research also shows that men and women in heterosexual marriages experience lower rates of domestic violence than people in any other living arrangement.

Do homosexuals pose a threat to children?

Homosexual men are far more likely to engage in child sexual abuse than are heterosexuals. The evidence for this lies in the findings that: Almost all child sexual abuse is committed by men; less than three percent of American men identify themselves as homosexual; yet nearly a third of all cases of child sexual abuse are homosexual in nature (that is, they involve men molesting boys). This is a rate of homosexual child abuse about ten times higher than one would expect based on the first two facts.

These figures are essentially undisputed. However, pro-homosexual activists seek to explain them away by claiming that men who molest boys are not usually homosexual in their adult sexual orientation. Yet a study of convicted child molesters, published in the *Archives of Sexual Behavior*, found that "86 percent of offenders against males described themselves as homosexual or bisexual" (W.D. Erickson, MD, et al., in *Archives of Sexual behavior* 17:1, 1988).

This does not mean that all, or even most, homosexual men are child molesters—but it does prove that homosexuality is a significant risk factor for this horrible crime.

But haven't studies shown that children raised by homosexual parents are no different from other children?

No. This claim is often put forward, even by professional organizations. The truth is that most research on "homosexual parents" thus far has been marred by serious methodological problems. However, even pro-homosexual sociologists Judith Stacey and Timothy Biblarz report that the actual data from key studies show the "no differences" claim to be false.

Surveying the research (primarily regarding lesbians) in an *American Sociological Review* article in 2001, they found that: Children of lesbians are less likely to conform to traditional gender norms; Children of lesbians are more likely to engage in homosexual behavior; Daughters of lesbians are "more sexually adventurous and less chaste"; Lesbian "co-parent relationships" are more likely to end than heterosexual ones.

A 1996 study by an Australian sociologist compared children raised by heterosexual married couples, heterosexual cohabiting couples, and homosexual cohabiting couples. It found that the children of heterosexual married couples did the best, and children of homosexual couples the worst, in nine of the thirteen academic and social categories measured.

What do these consequences of homosexual behavior have to do with marriage?

Since homosexual behavior is directly associated with higher rates of promiscuity, physical disease, mental illness, substance abuse, child sexual abuse, and domestic violence, there is no reason to reward such behavior by granting it society's ultimate affirmation—the status of civil marriage—or any of the benefits of marriage.

Do the American people want to see "marriages" between same-sex couples recognized by law?

No—and in the wake of the June 2003 court decisions to legalize such "marriages" in the Canadian province of Ontario and to legalize homosexual sodomy in the United States, the nation's opposition to such a radical social experiment has actually grown.

Five separate national opinion polls taken between June 24 and July 27, 2003, showed opponents of civil "marriage" for same-sex couples outnumbering supporters by not less than fifteen percentage points in every poll. The wording of poll questions can make a significant difference, and in this case, the poll with the most straightforward language (a Harris/CNN/Time poll asking "Do you think marriages between homosexual men or homosexual women should be recognized as legal by the law?") resulted in the strongest opposition, with 60 percent saying "No" and only 33 percent saying "Yes."

Even where pollsters drop the word "marriage" itself and use one of the euphemisms to describe a counterfeit institution parallel to marriage, we see a decline in public support for the homosexual agenda. The Gallup Poll, for instance, has asked, "Would you favor or oppose a law that would allow homosexual couples to legally form civil unions, giving them some of the legal rights of married couples?"

This question itself is misleading, in that it downplays the legal impact of "civil unions." Vermont, the only US state to adopt "civil unions" (under coercion of a state court), actually gives all "of the legal rights of married couples" available under state law to people in a same-sex "civil union"—not just "some." But despite this distortion, a 49-percent-to-49-percent split on this question in May 2003 had changed to opposition by a margin of 58 percent to 37 percent when the *Washington Post* asked the identical question in August 2003.

Even the percentage of Americans willing to declare that "homosexual relations between consenting adults" (never mind homosexual civil "marriage") "should be legal" dropped from 60 percent to only 48 percent between May and July of

2003. The biggest drop in support, a stunning 23 percentage points (from 58 percent to 35 percent), came among African Americans—despite the rhetoric of pro-homosexual activists who seek to frame the issues of "gay rights" and same-sex unions as a matter of "civil rights."

Is it necessary to amend the US Constitution to prevent legal recognition of civil "marriage" for same-sex couples?

No state legislature has even come close to allowing same-sex unions to be recognized as civil marriage. However, knowing that public opinion is firmly against them, pro-homosexual activists have now turned to the courts in an effort to get what they cannot achieve through the democratic process. Several states have heard lawsuits from same-sex couples demanding that they be granted marriage licenses, and at this writing there is a very real possibility that in the near future one or more state courts may order legal recognition of a same-sex civil "marriage."

If that happens, it is highly likely that some same-sex couples who obtain a civil "marriage" in that state will seek to have it recognized in other states. The 1996 Defense of Marriage Act (DOMA), which was passed by an overwhelming bipartisan majority in Congress and signed into law by President Clinton, declares that states do not have to recognize same-sex civil "marriages" contracted in other states. However, pro-homosexual activists would undoubtedly go to federal court to seek to have DOMA declared unconstitutional.

Such a legal challenge to DOMA ought to fail. But given the US Supreme Court's recent history of judicial activism on the subject of homosexuality, in defiance of the history and traditions of the country and even of the Court's own prior decisions, many have concluded that it would unsafe to trust the Court on this issue.

Amending the Constitution now appears to be the only way to achieve two indispensable goals: preserve a uniform national standard for something so fundamental to our civilization as the definition of marriage; and prevent the imposition of same-sex civil "marriage" or marital benefits through acts of undemocratic judicial tyranny.

Same-Sex Marriage Weakens the Institution of Marriage

Ryan T. Anderson

Ryan T. Anderson researches and writes about marriage and religious liberty as the William E. Simon Fellow at The Heritage Foundation, a conservative think tank based in Washington, DC.

At the heart of the current debates about same-sex marriage are three crucial questions: What is marriage, why does marriage matter for public policy, and what would be the consequences of redefining marriage to exclude sexual complementarity?

Marriage exists to bring a man and a woman together as husband and wife to be father and mother to any children their union produces. It is based on the anthropological truth that men and women are different and complementary, the biological fact that reproduction depends on a man and a woman, and the social reality that children need both a mother and a father. Marriage predates government. It is the fundamental building block of all human civilization. Marriage has public purposes that transcend its private purposes. This is why 41 states [at the time of this writing], with good reason, affirm that marriage is between a man and a woman.

Government recognizes marriage because it is an institution that benefits society in a way that no other relationship does. Marriage is society's least restrictive means of ensuring the well-being of children. State recognition of marriage protects children by encouraging men and women to commit to each other and take responsibility for their children. While respecting everyone's liberty, government rightly recognizes,

Ryan T. Anderson, "Marriage: What It Is, Why It Matters, and the Consequences of Redefining It," Backgrounder #2775 on Family and Marriage, Heritage Foundation, March 11, 2013. Copyright © 2013 by The Heritage Foundation. All rights reserved. Reproduced by permission.

protects, and promotes marriage as the ideal institution for childbearing and childrearing.

Promoting marriage does not ban any type of relationship: Adults are free to make choices about their relationships, and they do not need government sanction or license to do so. All Americans have the freedom to live as they choose, but no one has a right to redefine marriage for everyone else.

In recent decades, marriage has been weakened by a revisionist view that is more about adults' desires than children's needs. This reduces marriage to a system to approve emotional bonds or distribute legal privileges.

Redefining marriage to include same-sex relationships is the culmination of this revisionism, and it would leave emotional intensity as the only thing that sets marriage apart from other bonds. Redefining marriage would further distance marriage from the needs of children and would deny, as a matter of policy, the ideal that a child needs both a mom and a dad. Decades of social science, including the latest studies using large samples and robust research methods, show that children tend to do best when raised by a mother and a father. The confusion resulting from further delinking childbearing from marriage would force the state to intervene more often in family life and expand welfare programs. Redefining marriage would legislate a new principle that marriage is whatever emotional bond the government says it is.

Redefining marriage would destabilize marriage in ways that are known to hurt children.

Redefining marriage does not simply expand the existing understanding of marriage. It rejects the anthropological truth that marriage is based on the complementarity of man and woman, the biological fact that reproduction depends on a man and a woman, and the social reality that children need a mother and a father. Redefining marriage to abandon the norm of male-female sexual complementarity would also make other essential characteristics—such as monogamy, exclusivity, and permanency—optional. Marriage cannot do the work that society needs it to do if these norms are further weakened. . . .

The Consequences of Redefining Marriage

Redefining marriage would further disconnect childbearing from marriage. That would hurt children, especially the most vulnerable. It would deny as a matter of policy the ideal that children need a mother and a father. Traditional marriage laws reinforce the idea that a married mother and father is the most appropriate environment for rearing children, as the best available social science suggests.

Recognizing same-sex relationships as marriages would legally abolish that ideal. It would deny the significance of both mothering and fathering to children: that boys and girls tend to benefit from fathers and mothers in different ways. Indeed, the law, public schools, and media would teach that mothers and fathers are fully interchangeable and that thinking otherwise is bigoted.

Redefining marriage would diminish the social pressures and incentives for husbands to remain with their wives and *biological* children and for men and women to marry before having children. Yet the resulting arrangements—parenting by single parents, divorced parents, remarried parents, cohabiting couples, and fragmented families of any kind—are demonstrably worse for children. Redefining marriage would destabilize marriage in ways that are known to hurt children.

Leading LGBT advocates admit that redefining marriage changes its meaning. [*American Prospect* contributing editor] E. J. Graff celebrates the fact that redefining marriage would change the "institution's message" so that it would "ever after stand for sexual choice, for cutting the link between sex and diapers." Enacting same-sex marriage, she argues, "does more than just fit; it announces that marriage has changed shape."

[Political blogger] Andrew Sullivan says that marriage has become "primarily a way in which two adults affirm their emotional commitment to one another."

Redefining marriage is about cementing a new idea of marriage in the law.

Government exists to create the conditions under which individuals and freely formed communities can thrive. The most important free community—the one on which all others depend—is the marriage-based family. The conditions for its thriving include the accommodations and pressures that marriage law provides for couples to stay together. Redefining marriage would further erode marital norms, thrusting government further into leading roles for which it is poorly suited: parent and discipliner to the orphaned; provider to the neglected; and arbiter of disputes over custody, paternity, and visitation. As the family weakened, welfare programs and correctional bureaucracies would grow.

A Focus on Emotional Bond

Redefining marriage does not simply expand the existing understanding of marriage. It rejects the truth that marriage is based on the complementarity of man and woman, the biological fact that reproduction depends on a man and a woman, and the social reality that children need a mother and a father.

Redefining marriage to include same-sex relationships is not ultimately about expanding the pool of people who are eligible to marry. Redefining marriage is about cementing a new idea of marriage in the law—an idea whose baleful effects conservatives have fought for years. The idea that romantic-emotional union is all that makes a marriage cannot explain or support the stabilizing norms that make marriage fitting for family life. It can only undermine those norms.

Indeed, that undermining already has begun. Disastrous policies such as "no-fault" divorce were also motivated by the idea that a marriage is made by romantic attachment and satisfaction—and comes undone when these fade. Same-sex marriage would require a more formal and final redefinition of marriage as simple romantic companionship, obliterating the meaning that the marriage movement had sought to restore to the institution.

Weakening Marriage Norms

Government needs to get marriage policy right because it shapes the norms associated with this most fundamental relationship. Redefining marriage would abandon the norm of male-female sexual complementarity as an essential characteristic of marriage. Making that optional would also make other essential characteristics of marriage—such as monogamy, exclusivity, and permanency—optional. Weakening marital norms and severing the connection of marriage with responsible procreation are the admitted goals of many prominent advocates of redefining marriage.

The Norm of Monogamy

New York University Professor Judith Stacey has expressed hope that redefining marriage would give marriage "varied, creative, and adaptive contours," leading some to "question the dyadic limitations of Western marriage and seek . . . small group marriages." In their statement "Beyond Same-Sex Marriage," more than 300 "LGBT and allied" scholars and advocates call for legally recognizing sexual relationships involving more than two partners.

University of Calgary Professor Elizabeth Brake thinks that justice requires using legal recognition to "denormalize heterosexual monogamy as a way of life" and "rectif[y] past discrimination against homosexuals, bisexuals, polygamists, and care networks." She supports "minimal marriage," in which "individuals can have legal marital relationships with more than one person, reciprocally or asymmetrically, themselves determining the sex and number of parties, the type of relationship involved, and which rights and responsibilities to exchange with each."

In 2009, *Newsweek* reported that the United States already had over 500,000 polyamorous households. The author concluded:

> [P]erhaps the practice is more natural than we think: a response to the challenges of monogamous relationships, whose shortcomings . . . are clear. Everyone in a relationship wrestles at some point with an eternal question: can one person really satisfy every need? Polyamorists think the answer is obvious—and that it's only a matter of time before the monogamous world sees there's more than one way to live and love.

We often protest when homophobes insist that same sex marriage will change marriage for straight people too. But in some ways, they're right.

A 2012 article in *New York Magazine* introduced Americans to "throuple," a new term akin to a "couple," but with three people whose "throuplehood is more or less a permanent domestic arrangement. The three men work together, raise dogs together, sleep together, miss one another, collect art together, travel together, bring each other glasses of water, and, in general, exemplify a modern, adult relationship. Except that there are three of them."

The Norm of Exclusivity

Andrew Sullivan, who has extolled the "spirituality" of "anonymous sex," also thinks that the "openness" of same-sex unions could enhance the bonds of husbands and wives:

> Same-sex unions often incorporate the virtues of friendship more effectively than traditional marriages; and at times, among gay male relationships, the openness of the contract makes it more likely to survive than many heterosexual bonds.... [T]here is more likely to be greater understanding of the need for extramarital outlets between two men than between a man and a woman.... [S]omething of the gay relationship's necessary honesty, its flexibility, and its equality could undoubtedly help strengthen and inform many heterosexual bonds.

"Openness" and "flexibility" are Sullivan's euphemisms for sexual infidelity. Similarly, in a *New York Times Magazine* profile, gay activist Dan Savage encourages spouses to adopt "a more flexible attitude" about allowing each other to seek sex outside their marriage. *The New York Times* recently reported on a study finding that exclusivity was not the norm among gay partners: "'With straight people, it's called affairs or cheating,' said Colleen Hoff, the study's principal investigator, 'but with gay people it does not have such negative connotations.'"

A piece in *The Advocate* candidly admits where the logic of redefining marriage to include same-sex relationships leads:

> Anti-equality right-wingers have long insisted that allowing gays to marry will destroy the sanctity of "traditional marriage," and, of course, the logical, liberal party-line response has long been "No, it won't." But what if—for once—the sanctimonious crazies are right? Could the gay male tradition of open relationships actually alter marriage as we know it? And would that be such a bad thing?
>
> We often protest when homophobes insist that same sex marriage will change marriage for straight people too. But in some ways, they're right.

Weakening Marriage Is the Goal

Some advocates of redefining marriage embrace the goal of weakening the institution of marriage *in these very terms.*

"[Former President George W.] Bush is correct," says Victoria Brownworth, "when he states that allowing same-sex couples to marry will weaken the institution of marriage. . . . It most certainly will do so, and that will make marriage a far better concept than it previously has been." Professor Ellen Willis celebrates the fact that "conferring the legitimacy of marriage on homosexual relations will introduce an implicit revolt against the institution into its very heart."

Those who believe in monogamy and exclusivity—and the benefits that these bring to orderly procreation and child well-being—should take note.

[Radio talk-show host] Michelangelo Signorile urges same-sex couples to "demand the right to marry not as a way of adhering to society's moral codes but rather to debunk a myth and radically alter an archaic institution." Same-sex couples should "fight for same-sex marriage and its benefits and then, once granted, redefine the institution of marriage completely, because the most subversive action lesbians and gay men can undertake . . . is to transform the notion of 'family' entirely."

It is no surprise that there is already evidence of this occurring. A federal judge in Utah allowed a legal challenge to anti-bigamy laws. A bill that would allow a child to have three legal parents passed both houses of the California state legislature in 2012 before it was vetoed by the governor, who claimed he wanted "to take more time to consider all of the implications of this change." The impetus for the bill was a lesbian same-sex relationship in which one partner was impregnated by a man. The child possessed a biological mother and father, but the law recognized the biological mother and her same-sex spouse, a "presumed mother," as the child's parents.

Those who believe in monogamy and exclusivity—and the benefits that these bring to orderly procreation and child well-being—should take note.

Redefining Marriage Threatens Religious Liberty

Redefining marriage marginalizes those with traditional views and leads to the erosion of religious liberty. The law and culture will seek to eradicate such views through economic, social, and legal pressure. If marriage is redefined, believing what virtually every human society once believed about marriage—a union of a man and woman ordered to procreation and family life—would be seen increasingly as a malicious prejudice to be driven to the margins of culture. The consequences for religious believers are becoming apparent.

The administrative state may require those who contract with the government, receive governmental monies, or work directly for the state to embrace and promote same-sex marriage even if it violates their religious beliefs. Nondiscrimination law may make even private actors with no legal or financial ties to the government—including businesses and religious organizations—liable to civil suits for refusing to treat same-sex relationships as marriages. Finally, private actors in a culture that is now hostile to traditional views of marriage may discipline, fire, or deny professional certification to those who express support for traditional marriage.

The Becket Fund for Religious Liberty reports that "over 350 separate state anti-discrimination provisions would likely be triggered by recognition of same-sex marriage."

In fact, much of this is already occurring. Heritage Foundation Visiting Fellow Thomas Messner has documented multiple instances in which redefining marriage has already become a nightmare for religious liberty. If marriage is redefined to include same-sex relationships, then those who continue to believe the truth about marriage—that it is by nature a union of a man and a woman—would face three different types of threats to their liberty: the administrative state, nondiscrimination law, and private actors in a culture that is now hostile to traditional views.

After Massachusetts redefined marriage to include same-sex relationships, Catholic Charities of Boston was forced to discontinue its adoption services rather than place children with same-sex couples against its principles. Massachusetts public schools began teaching grade-school students about same-sex marriage, defending their decision because they are "committed to teaching about the world they live in, and in Massachusetts same-sex marriage is legal." A Massachusetts appellate court ruled that parents have no right to exempt their children from these classes.

The New Mexico Human Rights Commission prosecuted a photographer for declining to photograph a same-sex "commitment ceremony." Doctors in California were successfully sued for declining to perform an artificial insemination on a woman in a same-sex relationship. Owners of a bed and breakfast in Illinois who declined to rent their facility for a same-sex civil union ceremony and reception were sued for violating the state nondiscrimination law. A Georgia counselor was fired after she referred someone in a same-sex relationship to another counselor. In fact, the Becket Fund for Religious Liberty reports that "over 350 separate state anti-discrimination provisions would likely be triggered by recognition of same-sex marriage."

No Meaningful Protections

The Catholic bishop of Springfield, Illinois, explains how a bill, which was offered in that state's 2013 legislative session, to redefine marriage while claiming to protect religious liberty was unable to offer meaningful protections:

> [It] would not stop the state from obligating the Knights of Columbus to make their halls available for same-sex "weddings." It would not stop the state from requiring Catholic

grade schools to hire teachers who are legally "married" to someone of the same sex. This bill would not protect Catholic hospitals, charities, or colleges, which exclude those so "married" from senior leadership positions. . . . This "religious freedom" law does nothing at all to protect the consciences of people in business, or who work for the government. We saw the harmful consequences of deceptive titles all too painfully last year when the so-called "Religious Freedom Protection and Civil Union Act" forced Catholic Charities out of foster care and adoption services in Illinois.

For many supporters of redefining marriage, such infringements on religious liberty are not flaws but virtues of the movement.

In fact, the lack of religious liberty protection seems to be a feature of such bills:

There is no possible way—none whatsoever—for those who believe that marriage is exclusively the union of husband and wife to avoid legal penalties and harsh discriminatory treatment if the bill becomes law. Why should we expect it be otherwise? After all, we would be people who, according to the thinking behind the bill, hold onto an "unfair" view of marriage. The state would have equated our view with bigotry—which it uses the law to marginalize in every way short of criminal punishment.

Georgetown University law professor Chai Feldblum, an appointee to the U.S. Equal Employment Opportunity Commission, argues that the push to redefine marriage trumps religious liberty concerns:

[F]or all my sympathy for the evangelical Christian couple who may wish to run a bed and breakfast from which they can exclude unmarried, straight couples and all gay couples, this is a point where I believe the "zero-sum" nature of the game inevitably comes into play. And, in making that decision in this zero-sum game, I am convinced society should come down on the side of protecting the liberty of LGBT people.

Indeed, for many supporters of redefining marriage, such infringements on religious liberty are not flaws but virtues of the movement.

The Future of Marriage

Long before the debate about same-sex marriage, there was a debate about marriage. It launched a "marriage movement" to explain why marriage was good both for the men and women who were faithful to its responsibilities and for the children they reared. Over the past decade, a new question emerged: What does society have to lose by redefining marriage to exclude sexual complementarity?

Government recognizes traditional marriage because it benefits society in a way that no other relationship or institution does.

Many citizens are increasingly tempted to think that marriage is simply an intense emotional union, whatever sort of interpersonal relationship consenting adults, whether two or 10 in number, want it to be—sexual or platonic, sexually exclusive or open, temporary or permanent. This leaves marriage with no essential features, no fixed core as a social reality. It is simply whatever consenting adults want it to be.

Yet if marriage has no form and serves no social purpose, how will society protect the needs of children—the prime victim of our non-marital sexual culture—without government growing *more* intrusive and *more* expensive?

Marriage exists to bring a man and a woman together as husband and wife to be father and mother to any children their union produces. Marriage benefits everyone because separating the bearing and rearing of children from marriage burdens innocent bystanders: not just children, but the whole community. Without healthy marriages, the community often must step in to provide (more or less directly) for their well-being and upbringing. Thus, by encouraging the norms of marriage—monogamy, sexual exclusivity, and permanence—the state strengthens civil society and reduces its own role.

Government recognizes traditional marriage because it benefits society in a way that no other relationship or institution does. Marriage is society's least restrictive means of ensuring the well-being of children. State recognition of marriage protects children by encouraging men and women to commit to each other and take responsibility for their children.

Promoting marriage does not ban any type of relationship: Adults are free to make choices about their relationships, and they do not need government sanction or license to do so. All Americans have the freedom to live as they choose, but no one has a right to redefine marriage for everyone else.

The future of this country depends on the future of marriage, and the future of marriage depends on citizens understanding what it is and why it matters and demanding that government policies support, not undermine, true marriage.

Some might appeal to historical inevitability as a reason to avoid answering the question of what marriage is—as if it were an already moot question. However, changes in public opinion are driven by human choice, not by blind historical forces. The question is not what will happen, but what we should do.

Same-Sex Marriage Perpetuates Systemic Injustices

Dean Spade and Craig Willse

Dean Spade is an associate professor at the Seattle University School of Law and is currently a fellow in the Engaging Tradition Project at Columbia Law School. He is the author of Normal Life: Administrative Violence, Critical Trans Politics and the Limits of Law. *Craig Willse is an assistant professor of cultural studies at George Mason University in Virginia. He is co-editor of* Beyond Biopolitics: Essays on the Governance of Life and Death.

*T*hat *marriage is a failure none but the very stupid will deny.*

—Emma Goldman

In recent years, lots of progressive people have been celebrating marriage—when various states have passed laws recognizing same-sex marriage, when courts have made decisions affirming the legal recognition of same-sex marriage, when politicians have spoken in favor of it. At the same time, many queer activists and scholars have relentlessly critiqued same-sex marriage advocacy. Supporters of marriage sometimes acknowledge those critiques, and respond with something like: While marriage is not for everyone, and won't solve everything, we still need it.

What's the deal? Is same-sex marriage advocacy a progressive cause? Is it in line with Left political projects of racial and economic justice, decolonization, and feminist liberation?

Nope. Same-sex marriage advocacy has accomplished an amazing feat—it has made being anti-homophobic synonymous with being pro-marriage. It has drowned out centuries of critical thinking and activism against the racialized, colonial, and patriarchal processes of state regulation of family and gender through marriage. It is to such an understanding of marriage we first turn.

What Is Marriage?

Civil marriage is a tool of social control used by governments to regulate sexuality and family formation by establishing a favored form and rewarding it (in the U.S., for example, with over one thousand benefits). While marriage is being rewarded, other ways of organizing family, relationships and sexual behavior do not receive these benefits and are stigmatized and criminalized. In short, people are punished or rewarded based on whether or not they marry. The idea that same-sex marriage advocacy is a fight for the "freedom to marry" or "equality" is absurd since the existence of legal marriage is a form of coercive regulation in which achieving or not achieving marital status is linked to accessing vital life resources like health care and paths to legalized immigration. There is nothing freeing nor equalizing about such a system. . . .

Forcing indigenous people to comply with European norms of gender, sexuality and family structure and punishing them for not doing so has been a key tool of US settler colonialism in North America.

Societal myths about marriage, which are replicated in same-sex marriage advocacy, tell us that marriage is about love, about care for elders and children, about sharing the good life together—even that it is the cornerstone of a happy personal life and a healthy civilization. Feminist, anti-racist, and anti-colonial social movements have contested this, identifying marriage as a system that violently enforces sexual and familial norms. From these social movements, we understand marriage as a technology of social control, exploitation, and dispossession wrapped in a satin ribbon of sexist and hetero-patriarchal romance mythology.

Marriage Is a Tool of Anti-Black Racism

Since the founding of the US, regulating family formation has been key to anti-Black racism and violence. Denying the family ties of slaves was essential to slavery—ensuring that children would be born enslaved and maintaining Black people as property rather than persons. After emancipation, the government scrambled to control Black people, coercing marriage among newly freed Black people and criminalizing them for adultery as one pathway of recapturing them into the convict lease system. After *Brown v. Board of Education*, which challenged formal, legal segregation, illegitimacy laws became a favored way to exclude Black children from programs and services. The idea that married families and their children are superior was and remains a key tool of anti-Black racism.

Black families have consistently been portrayed as pathological and criminal in academic research and social policy based on marriage rates, most famously in the Moynihan Report. Anti-poor and anti-Black discourse and policymaking frame poverty as a result of the lack of marriage in Black populations. [Former President Bill] Clinton's 1996 dismantling of welfare programs, which disproportionately harmed Black families, was justified by an explicit discourse about poverty resulting from unmarried parenthood. Under both President George W. Bush and President Barack Obama, "Health Marriage Promotion" initiatives have been used to encourage low-income women to marry, including at times through cash incentives. Demonizing, managing and controlling Black people by applying racist and sexist marital family norms to justify both brutal interventions and "benign neglect" has a long history in the US and remains standard fare.

Marriage Is a Tool of Colonialism

Colonization often casts invasion as rescuing colonized populations from their backward gender and family systems. We can see this from the land we're writing this on (Washington, D.C. & Washington State) to Afghanistan. Forcing indigenous people to comply with European norms of gender, sexuality and family structure and punishing them for not doing so has been a key tool of US settler colonialism in North America. Marriage has been an important tool of land theft and ethnic cleansing aimed at disappearing indigenous people in many ways. The US encouraged westward settlement by promising male settlers 160 acres to move west, plus an extra 160 if they married and brought a wife. At the same time, the US criminalized traditional indigenous communal living styles, burning longhouses where indigenous people lived communally, eliminating communal landholding methods, and enforcing male individual ownership. Management of gender and family systems was and is essential to displacement and settlement processes. Enforcing gender norms in boarding schools as part of a "civilizing mission," and removing children from native communities through a variety of programs that persist today are key tools of ethnic cleansing and settlement in the US.

Marriage has always been about who is whose property (women, slaves, children) and who gets what property.

Marriage Is a Tool of Xenophobia and Immigration Enforcement

From its origins, US immigration law has put in place mechanisms for regulating those migrants it does allow in, always under threat of deportation, and labeling other migrants "undesirable" to both make them more exploitable by their bosses and easier to purge. Keeping out poor people, people with stigmatized health issues, and people of color have been urgent national priorities. Marriage has been one of the key valves of that control. The Page Act of 1875, for example, sought to keep out Asian women, hoping to prevent Asian laborers in the US from reproducing, but allowed the immigration of Asian merchants' wives. Marriage continues to be a deeply unjust tool of immigration control in the US, with marital family ties being one of the few pathways to immigration. One impact of this system is that it keeps people stuck in violent and harmful sexual and family relationships because their immigration status depends on it.

Marriage Is a Tool of Gendered Social Control

Feminists have long understood marriage as a tool of social control and labor exploitation. This is why feminists have worked to dismantle the mystique around romance, marriage, child rearing and care—exposing these as cultural fantasies that coerce women into unpaid labor and cultivate sexual violence. They have also worked to change laws to make it easier to get out of marriages, and to de-link marital status from essential things people need (like immigration and health care) because those links trap women and children in violent family relationships.

Marriage Is About Protecting Private Property and Ensuring Maldistribution

Marriage has always been about who is whose property (women, slaves, children) and who gets what property. Inheritance, employee benefits, insurance claims, taxation, wrongful death claims—all of the benefits associated with marriage are benefits that keep wealth in the hands of the wealthy. Those with no property are less likely to marry, and have less to protect using marriage law. Movements for economic justice are about dismantling property systems that keep people poor—

not tinkering with them so that people with wealth can use them more effectively to protect their wealth.

Today's same-sex marriage advocates argue in courts and in the media that marriage is the bedrock of our society, that children need and deserve married parents, and that marriage is the most important relationship people can have. These arguments are the exact opposite of what feminist, anti-racist and anti-colonial movements have been saying for hundreds of years as they sought to dismantle state marriage because of its role in maldistributing life chances and controlling marginalized populations.

Responses to Critiques of Same-Sex Marriage Advocacy

You don't have to get married if you don't want to.

Same-sex marriage has been framed through a paradigm of "choice," that some of us can do this if we want to, and those that don't want to should back off and let us plan our weddings already. But such choices take place in a field of limited options already structured by legal and cultural systems. Coercive systems distribute rewards and punishments— marriage punishes those who do not participate in it. Saying that marriage is an individual choice hides this. Marriage is part of a system where the government chooses some relationships, family structures and sexual behaviors as the gold standard and rewards them, while others are stigmatized and/or criminalized. . . .

Same-sex marriage advocacy has bolstered conservative mythologies about how marriage is about love and is the best way to have a family.

But marriage is about love and love is revolutionary!

As described above, marriage is about controlling people and property for the benefit of white people, wealthy people

155

and settlers. It does so under the cover of a consumer-driven mythology about love. US popular culture is permeated by a set of myths about sex and romance that feminists have long worked to analyze and dismantle. We are told that people, but especially women, have empty, useless lives unless they are married. Women are encouraged to feel scarcity about the ability to marry—to feel that they better find the right person and convince him to marry them quickly—or else face an empty life. In this equation, women are valued only for conforming to racist and sexist body norms and men are also objectified and ranked according to wealth. These myths drive the diet industry, much of the entertainment industry, and certainly the gigantic wedding industry ($40 billion per year in the US), which is based on people's terrified attempts to appear as wealthy, skinny, and normative as possible for one heavily documented day. Feminists understand the scarcity and insecurity that women are trained to experience about love, romance and marriage as a form of coercion, pushing women into exploitative and abusive sexual relationships and family roles. Media messaging about how essential marriage and childrearing is for women to have a meaningful life is part of an ongoing conservative backlash against feminist work that sought to free women from violence and unpaid domestic labor.

This does not mean that people do not experience love in many ways, including in romantic relationships. But the system of marriage is not about the government wanting to recognize people's love and support it—it is about controlling people and resources. Same-sex marriage advocacy has bolstered conservative mythologies about how marriage is about love and is the best way to have a family.

But if I want to express my love this way, stop telling me how to be queer!

One common response to critiques of same-sex marriage advocacy is defensiveness by those who are married or want to be married. These people often claim to feel judged by the critics. This response, reducing a systemic critique to a feeling of discomfort about being individually judged, is so disappointing coming from anyone on the Left! Haven't we learned to recognize that we are implicated in oppressive systems, and even benefit from them? Don't we know how to hear a critique of a system that we're implicated in and realize that we should not silence it to dispel our discomfort, or pretend to be victimized by the critique because it is hard to recognize our own privilege? Okay, we're not great at it, but let's work on that. It is absurd for married people or people who want to marry to paint themselves as victims of judgment when someone critiques the institution of marriage while the entire society is organized to support them for marrying. . . .

Legalizing same-sex marriage puts a stamp of "equality" on systems that remain brutally harmful, because a few more-privileged people will get something from the change.

But it will get people health care and immigration status.

Why should anyone have to get married to get health care or immigration status? Same-sex marriage advocacy is sold as a method of getting people vitally needed resources, but most undocumented queer people don't have a partner who is a citizen and most uninsured/unemployed queer people don't have a partner with a job with health benefits. People tend to date in their own class statuses so we cannot partner our way out of immigration and health care crises, nor is it acceptable for our movements to endorse that kind of coercion. Same-sex marriage advocacy is not a strategy for really attacking these problems. At best it helps a few of the most privileged get these necessities, but those in the worst circumstances see no change. . . .

It is unethical for movements to prioritize those with the most access. We should prioritize those vulnerable to the most severe manifestations of homophobia and transphobia. That would mean putting resources toward real solutions to these problems—the struggles against immigration enforcement and for health care access for all—and bringing particular insight about homophobia and transphobia to these struggles. Legalizing same-sex marriage puts a stamp of "equality" on systems that remain brutally harmful, because a few more-privileged people will get something from the change. . . .

But queers will change marriage.

When people say this they are often referring to how the traditional gender roles of "husband" and "wife" will be altered by the possibility of having two women or two men as married spouses. The problem is, we already know how sadly little difference this will make. We know that queer relationships have the same rates of domestic violence (approx 30%) as straight relationships.

We know that adding women or queers or people of color to roles where they were traditionally excluded, such as police forces or militaries, does not change those roles or the institutions that rely on them. The argument that adding same-sex couples to marriage will "change marriage" is based on a hope for cultural shift that not only fails to address that the harmful, racist and colonial structures of marriage stay firmly in place, but also ignores that same-sex marriage advocacy has produced a much stronger cultural shift that has beat back feminist and anti-racist critiques of marriage and re-valorized marriage with a romantic mystique.

The Realm of Culture

Further, this argument for same-sex marriage advocacy locates marriage only in the realm of culture. Of course, culture and economy interact in complex ways, and changing cultural norms about gender and sexuality is not irrelevant. Shifting cultural norms often comes with economic rewards and opportunities, for those whose status is shifted. While same-sex marriage legalization may shift the "meaning of marriage" in some symbolic ways, in no way at all does it undo the damage produced by the institution as it distributes its rewards and punishments. It just gives some of those rewards to some more people—same-sex couples with property to share, health benefits to share, and/or immigration status to share might gain something, but the growing numbers of queer and trans people who are poor, unemployed, undocumented and/or uninsured will see no change. It also further legitimizes the punishment of those who are excluded by branding marriage as inclusive and just—so it must be your fault you're all alone and have no health insurance!!

Legalizing same-sex marriage is not an incremental step toward what queer and trans people need to reduce the harm and violence we face, it's a moment when that harm is being publicly officially resolved while in reality it worsens.

Some people also argue that same-sex marriage advocacy has improved popular opinion about gay and lesbian people, helping more people see gay and lesbian people as members of families, as parents, as ordinary couples rather than through hyper-sexualized or pathologizing stereotypes. The problem with the limited newfound acceptance won by this advocacy is that it hinges on portraying queer people as members of normative couples, reifying the stigmatization of everyone who is not. Queer politics should be about dismantling the sexual and gender hierarchies; same-sex marriage efforts are about getting those who can conform into the charmed circle. This couples' rights framework not only fails to challenge, but is actually aligned with, the ongoing expansion of criminalization of queer and trans people through sex offender registries, sex trafficking statutes and other recent tools of criminalization. Inventing a new inaccurate stereotype—one that portrays queer people as just a bunch of domesticated normative couples—is a terrible strategy if our goal is to reduce the harms wrought by systems of sexual and gender coercion and violence.

But what you want is unwinnable—we need to take incremental steps and this is an incremental step towards equality.

This is a heartbreakingly conservative argument that says there is no alternative to neoliberalism, to capitalism, to a culture based on racist criminalization and imprisonment. We are relentlessly told not to imagine alternatives, and only to tinker with hideous systems to let a few more people in. Legalizing same-sex marriage is not an incremental step toward what queer and trans people need to reduce the harm and violence we face, it's a moment when that harm is being publicly officially resolved while in reality it worsens. The "deserving" and "undeserving" are further divided, and the institution of marriage and its mystique are rehabilitated in the name of anti-homophobia.

Same-sex marriage advocacy celebrates and promotes marriage, abandons all those punished by marriage systems, and tells us that while we shouldn't get in the way of your wedding, we certainly can't expect any solidarity from you.

Against Inclusion

Same-sex marriage advocacy has been harmful just like other political strategies that seek inclusion in a violent state apparatus—such as the fight for gay and lesbian military service. Inclusion strategies like these valorize the things they seek inclusion in. Same-sex marriage advocacy has lined up with right wing family values rhetoric and policy to undo the work of our movements to gradually dismantle marriage and separate access to key necessities from marital status. It has aligned with conservative pro-marriage ideas about romance, children, families and care that support the attacks on social welfare programs and most severely harm low-income mothers of color. It has rescued marriage from Left critique and made straight and gay people on the Left forget what our movements have taught us about state regulation of families and gender.

Inclusion arguments also require their advocates to divide their constituencies by producing narratives about how "we deserve to be included." This has meant producing a world of representations of gay and lesbian couples who are monogamous, upper class, tax-paying, obedient consumers. The stories have to focus on those who have something to lose from not being able to marry—the white European immigrants America should want, the couples who want to boost our economy with expensive weddings, the people with wealth to pass on when they die. The promotion of this image of queer life and queer people as "rights deserving" couples who meet America's racial, class and moral norms participates in the relentless demonizing of all those cast out of the charmed circle—especially all the queer and trans people facing criminalization for poverty, participation in the sex trade, homelessness, and all those who will not reap the rewards of legal marriage.

The Marriage-Advocacy Machine

We have been told that same-sex marriage is a grassroots movement, but this is not the case. The decision to produce the giant machine of same-sex marriage advocacy that crowds out from public view all the other anti-homophobic and anti-transphobic grassroots work happening in the US came from the top. The world of well-resourced gay rights organizations and the few wealthy foundations and donors who fund them is tiny—the gay 1%. Its agenda is made behind closed doors, and queer and trans 99%-ers only get to be reactive to these strategies, as their lives and demands are framed by corporate media and the gay elite. Some eat it up, others talk back, but ultimately, we get no say. Perhaps if the same-sex marriage advocacy story is good for anything, it's as a great illustration of the power of philanthropy to shape a movement. We have seen what some say started at street rebellions against police violence at the Stonewall Inn and Compton's Cafeteria turn into advocacy for prosecution and partnership with police. We have seen a movement birthed during and because of the radical politics of anti-war and decolonization resistance of the 1960's and 70's become focused on the right to serve in the US military. And we have seen the eclipse of queer, feminist, anti-racist and decolonial critiques of government regulation of sexuality and family norms evolve into a demand to get married under the law. It is stunning to watch, in such a short period, the rebranding of institutions of state violence as sites of freedom and equality. As the same-sex marriage fight draws to a close in the coming years and conditions remain brutal for queer and trans people without wealth, immigration status or health care, it is vitally important that we support and expand the racial and economic justice centered queer and trans activism that has never seen marriage as an answer.

CHAPTER 3

Current
CONTROVERSIES

Is Same-Sex Marriage Good for Families and Children?

Overview: Gay Couples Weigh Financial Options That Accompany Marriage

Martha M. Hamilton

Martha M. Hamilton is a business columnist at The Washington Post.

Refreshed by a late September vacation in Canada, Beth McKinnon and Ann Carper were ready for the job ahead—figuring out whether it makes sense to get married as a result of the Supreme Court's summer [2013] ruling on the Defense of Marriage Act.

The women have been together since 1998, and they have already tied the knot in two ways, a civil union in 2001 in Vermont and a domestic partnership filed in the District [of Columbia], where they live. "We feel married in the eyes of our friends and family," Carper said.

But now that they could also be married in the eyes of the federal government, that might change the equation. And it's an equation with many parts. The ruling that struck down the federal law known as DOMA [Defense of Marriage Act] and subsequent regulations issued by the Internal Revenue Service and other federal agencies mean that same-sex spouses are now eligible for many benefits they were previously denied.

But they also might get hit hard by taxes if marrying and filing jointly increases their tax brackets. That's what McKinnon and Carper hope to sort through in the next few weeks.

If they get married, "it would really be for financial reasons, as unromantic as it sounds," said Carper, sitting at a kitchen table next to a window that overlooks their flower and vegetable gardens.

Not everyone takes that analytic approach.

For many couples, the romantic impulse took over, but when financial planner Tom Tillery's clients called saying they were rushing off to where it was legal to marry, he said he held up a stop sign.

"For our gay and lesbian clients, it was heartbreaking," said Tillery, who has clients around the country, recounting a conversation with a client who called excitedly after the ruling to say she was flying to New York to marry her partner.

Tillery and others recommend what Carper and McKinnon are doing—taking the time required to sort out the financial implications. After the ruling "the biggest complication was laying myself in front of the train of my clients wanting to run off and get married," said Tillery, whose firm, Paraklete Financial, is based in Kennesaw, Ga.

One major question to be answered is what the Social Security Administration will do [with regard to same-sex marriages].

The federal government has been relatively quick to issue rulings based on the decision. The Office of Personnel Management and the Pentagon extended benefits to the spouses married where same-sex unions are legal, while the Department of Homeland Security recognized such marriages as the basis for immigration. The Defense Department also extended 10 days' leave to members of the military planning to marry, to make it easier to travel to where same-sex marriages may be legally celebrated.

On Aug. 29, the IRS followed in those agencies' footsteps, ruling that same-sex couples legally married in jurisdictions that recognize their marriages will be treated as married for federal tax purposes.

"This ruling also assures legally married same-sex couples that they can move freely throughout the country knowing that their federal filing status will not change," Treasury Secretary Jacob Lew said. On Sept. 4, Attorney General Eric H. Holder Jr. advised congressional leaders that President Obama had directed the Department of Veterans Affairs to provide benefits to spouses in same-sex marriages despite a federal statute that limits spousal benefits to spouses of the opposite sex.

What About Social Security?

One major question to be answered is what the Social Security Administration will do. It bases spousal benefits on a couple's place of residence, rather than where the marriage was performed. Even so, when it comes to Social Security, experts are advising individuals to apply for spousal and survivor benefits as soon as they can, because the benefits, once approved, are retroactive to the date of application. Social Security has encouraged not just same-sex married couples but also couples in other legally recognized relationships such as civil unions and registered domestic partnerships to apply.

According to Patricia A. Cain, a tax professor at Santa Clara University and a national expert on sexuality and the law, the IRS ruling was timely because many taxpayers had postponed filing their 2012 taxes by asking for extensions, and the decision came through before the Oct. 15 deadline.

Among other complications when it comes to federal income taxes, couples will have to decide whether to amend separately filed individual returns for the past three years, based on whether they would pay more. As a rule of thumb, two individuals who both earn relatively high incomes would likely be worse off by amending returns, because of the possibility of a higher tax rate applied to the pooled earnings, while a couple with one high-earning individual and another who is lower income might benefit from bracket-lowering dilution.

On the other hand, a dual high-earning couple might still want to marry to qualify for the marital exemption or deduction from estate taxes. While federal estate taxes apply only to estates in excess of $5.25 million, 21 states and the District have estate taxes, most of which kick in at $1 million. Although the ruling on DOMA doesn't affect those laws, it's a consideration for some couples in deciding whether to get married.

Considering Eventualities

You could try timing it to get the best of both worlds, said Laurie Kane Burkhardt, a financial planner for Modera Wealth Management, which has offices in Massachusetts and New Jersey. "If you're going to stay with someone for the rest of your life and have enough assets that your partner might end up paying the estate tax, you may not want to get married until later in life," she said. Of course, the risk is that "you can't time dying."

One other major consideration couples should take into account is what happens in the event of divorce.

And, in the case of a couple with a large earnings discrepancy, if the low-earning individual receives any assistance based on income, such as the earned income tax credit or federal subsidies to help reduce the cost of insurance bought in the recently opened health-care exchanges, filing jointly might reduce or eliminate those benefits.

Then there is the issue of taxes paid before 2013. Taxpayers are allowed to refile taxes and claim refunds going back three years.

One other major consideration couples should take into account is what happens in the event of divorce, said Susan Sommer, director of constitutional litigation for Lambda Legal. "One thing for people to remember is that, while there is no residency requirement to get married to a same-sex spouse [in jurisdictions that recognize them], there generally are residency requirements to get divorced." Of the places where same-sex marriages are permitted, the District, California, Delaware, Minnesota and Vermont allow couples who were married there but live elsewhere to divorce under their laws, although Vermont has some limits.

Federal Worker Benefits

Although clearing up the financial calculus will take time and probably result in additional litigation, there are some couples for whom getting married is much more clearly a winning strategy, said Jerry Cannizzaro, a financial planner with the Reston-based firm Ticknor Atherton & Associates. They are couples in which one member is a federal worker. "Federal government employees are in a great situation" because federal benefits are so good, he said.

"The federal government has guaranteed health insurance for life," Cannizzaro said. The surviving spouse is covered even after a retired federal employee dies, he said. The surviving spouse would also be entitled to a percentage of the worker's retirement annuity.

Cannizzaro's clients include Carper, who is a federal employee, and McKinnon, who is a retired Social Security manager. McKinnon is thinking through how it would work if she went back and opted for survivor benefits that she didn't take when she retired. Her pension would be reduced, but Carper would receive benefits if she outlived McKinnon.

That's one of the issues that the women, who both describe themselves as practical and frugal, will be discussing with Cannizzaro—and with their accountant and an estate attorney.

While waiting for the details to be sorted out after the DOMA decision, activists are moving the fight for marriage equality into the states. "We're still living in a patchwork country where rights are far from complete," said Lambda Legal's Sommer. "We're in a state of incremental equality. It's far better than where we were a few months ago, but we still have a way to go."

Same-Sex Marriage Protects Families and Children in Many Ways

Marriage Equality USA

Marriage Equality USA is a volunteer-driven national nonprofit whose mission is to secure legally recognized civil marriage equality for all, without regard to sexual orientation or gender identity.

Marriage equality is an issue that often sparks intense emotions, both in those who are working for equality, and in those who oppose it. The institution of marriage is also surrounded by a great deal of assumption and mythology. It behooves us all to get the facts before discussing marriage equality. . . .

Marriage offers many legal benefits and responsibilities that protect families. It also provides societal status and emotional benefits. Here are just a fraction of the reasons why marriage matters to couples who choose/desire to marry.

The Practical

Marriage offers 1,138 Federal benefits and responsibilities, not including hundreds more offered by every state.

- In times of crisis, spouses have hospital visitation rights and can make medical decisions in event of illness or disability of their spouse.

- Employers offer spouses sick leave, bereavement leave, access to health insurance and pension.

- The law provides certain automatic rights to a person's spouse regardless of whether or not a will exists.

- Married couples in elderly care facilities are generally not separated unless one spouse's health dictates hospitalization or special care.

- The dissolution of a marriage requires a determination of property distribution, award of child custody and support and spousal support. Absent divorce, there is no uniform system for sorting out the ending of a relationship.

The Financial

Financial issues are complex and challenging, no matter the couple. When home ownership, kids and other assets are a part of the equation, planning for the present and especially the future is even more critical for greater security.

- Married couples are permitted to give an unlimited amount of gifts to each other without being taxed.

- The law presumes that a married couple with both names on the title to their home owns the property as "tenants by the entirety."

- A married couple, by statute, has creditor protection of their marital home.

- Many married people are entitled to financial benefits relating to their spouses, such as disability, pension and social security benefits.

- With marriage, a couple has the right to be treated as an economic unit and to file joint tax returns (and pay the marriage penalty), and obtain joint health, home and auto insurance policies.

- When a spouse dies, there is no need to prove owner-ship of every item in the household for taxable purposes.

Parenting by same-gender couples is an established and growing part of the diverse structure of families in the United States.

Protecting Children

- A child who grows up with married parents benefits from the fact that his or her parents' relationship is recognized by law and receives legal protections.

- Spouses are generally entitled to joint child custody and visitation upon divorce (and bear an obligation to pay child support).

- The mark of a strong family and healthy children is having parents who are nurturing, caring, and loving. Parents should be judged on their ability to parent, not by their age, race, religion, gender, disability, sexual orientation or gender identity.

A study published in the *Journal of the American Academy of Pediatrics*, entitled "The Effects of Marriage, Civil Union, and Domestic Partnership Laws on the Health and Well-being of Children," found that:

- Same-gender couples live in 99.3% of all US counties.

- Same-gender couples are raising children in at least 96% of all US counties.

- Nearly one quarter of all same-gender couples are raising children.

- Nationwide, 34.3% of lesbian couples are raising children, and 22.3% of gay male couples are raising children (compared with 45.6% of married heterosexual and 43.1% of unmarried heterosexual couples raising children).

- Vermont has the largest aggregation of same gender-couples ($\sim$1% of all households) followed by California, Washington, Massachusetts, and Oregon.

According to [a] 2006 study Census 2000 and related demographic research make it clear that parenting by same-gender couples is an established and growing part of the diverse structure of families in the United States. Public policies that aim to promote family stability and security typically are established without consideration for same-gender parents and their children, and they place these families at a disadvantage, as they do heterosexual unmarried parents, single parents, and extended-family caregivers. Public policy designed to promote the family as the basic building block of society has at its core the protection of children's health and well-being. Children's well-being relies in large part on a complex blend of their own legal rights and the rights derived, under law, from their parents. Children of same-gender parents often experience economic, legal, and familial insecurity as a result of the absence of legal recognition of their bonds to their non-biological parents. Current public-policy trends, with notable exceptions, favor limiting or prohibiting the availability of civil marriage and limiting rights and protections to same-gender couples.

The Healthy Advantage

Studies show that people who are married tend to live longer and lead healthier lives.

- For adults, a stable, happy marriage is the best protector against illness and premature death. Decades of research have clearly established these links.

173

- Studies on marriages have found that married people live longer, have higher incomes and wealth, engage less in risky behaviors, eat healthier, and have fewer psychological problems than unmarried people.

- Research shows that unmarried couples have lower levels of happiness and well-being than married couples.

- A recent study shows that denying same-sex couples the right to marry has a negative impact on their mental health.

There Is No Scientific Evidence That Same-Sex Marriage Harms Children

Nathalie F.P. Gilfoyle

Nathalie F.P. Gilfoyle is general counsel for the American Psychological Association, a 130,000-member nonprofit association representing psychologists in the United States.

Like their heterosexual counterparts, many gay men and lesbians desire to form stable, long-lasting, committed relationships. Substantial numbers are successful in doing so. Empirical studies using nonrepresentative samples of gay men and lesbians show that the vast majority of participants have been involved in a committed relationship at some point in their lives, that large proportions are currently involved in such a relationship (across studies, roughly 40–70% of gay men and 45–80% of lesbians), and that a substantial number of those couples have been together 10 or more years. Recent surveys based on more representative samples of gay men, lesbians, and bisexuals support these findings and indicate that many same-sex couples are cohabiting. An analysis of data from the 2000 US Census reported that same-sex couples headed more than 92,000 California households. More recent Census data indicate that the number of reported same-sex cohabiting couples in California was approximately 107,700 in 2005.

Empirical research demonstrates that the psychological and social aspects of committed relationships between same-sex partners closely resemble those of heterosexual partner-

Nathalie F.P. Gilfoyle, "Brief of the American Psychological Association, The California Psychological Association, The American Psychiatric Association, and The American Association of Marriage and Family Therapy as Amici Curiae in Support of Plaintiff-Appellees," United States Court of Appeals for the Ninth Circuit, October 27, 2010.

ships. Like heterosexual couples, same-sex couples form deep emotional attachments and commitments. Heterosexual and same-sex couples alike face similar challenges concerning issues such as intimacy, love, equity, loyalty, and stability, and they go through similar processes to address those challenges. Empirical research examining the quality of intimate relationships also shows that gay and lesbian couples have similar or higher levels of relationship satisfaction than do heterosexual couples.

Based on the empirical research findings, the American Psychological Association has concluded that "[p]sychological research on relationships and couples provides no evidence to justify discrimination against same-sex couples." . . .

A large and ever increasing number of gay and lesbian couples, like their heterosexual counterparts, raise children together. Although data are not available to indicate the exact number of lesbian and gay parents in the United States, the 2000 Census found that, among the 92,000 California household heads who reported cohabiting with a same-sex partner, 33% of women and 20% of men had a son or daughter under 18 living in their home. Because the U.S. Census does not capture all sexual minority partners, researchers estimate that considerably more parents today identify themselves as gay, lesbian, or bisexual.

Gays and Lesbians Are Fit Parents

Although it is sometimes asserted in policy debates that heterosexual couples are inherently better parents than same-sex couples, or that the children of lesbian or gay parents fare worse than children raised by heterosexual parents, those assertions find no support in the scientific research literature.

When comparing the outcomes of different forms of parenting, it is critically important to make appropriate comparisons. For example, differences resulting from the *number* of parents in a household cannot be attributed to the parents' *gender* or *sexual orientation*. Research in households with heterosexual parents generally indicates that—all else being equal—children do better with two parenting figures rather than just one. The specific research studies typically cited in this regard do not address parents' sexual orientation, however, and therefore do not permit any conclusions to be drawn about the consequences of having heterosexual versus nonheterosexual parents, or two parents who are of the same versus different genders.

Every relevant study to date shows that parental sexual orientation per se has no measurable effect on the quality of parent-child relationships or on children's mental health or social adjustment.

Indeed, the scientific research that has directly compared outcomes for children with gay and lesbian parents with outcomes for children with heterosexual parents has been consistent in showing that lesbian and gay parents are as fit and capable as heterosexual parents, and their children are as psychologically healthy and well-adjusted as children reared by heterosexual parents. Empirical research over the past two decades has failed to find any meaningful differences in the parenting ability of lesbian and gay parents compared to heterosexual parents. Most research on this topic has focused on lesbian mothers and refutes the stereotype that lesbian parents are not as child-oriented or maternal as non-lesbian mothers. Researchers have concluded that heterosexual and lesbian mothers do not differ in their parenting ability. Relatively few studies have directly examined gay fathers, but those that exist find that gay men are similarly fit and able parents, as compared to heterosexual men.

Children of Gay Parents Fare Well

Turning to the children of gay parents, researchers reviewing the scientific literature conclude that studies "provide no evidence that psychological adjustment among lesbians, gay men, their children, or other family members is impaired in any significant way" and that "every relevant study to date shows that parental sexual orientation per se has no measurable effect on the quality of parent-child relationships or on children's mental health or social adjustment." A comprehensive survey of peer-reviewed scientific studies in this area reported no differences between children raised by lesbians and those raised by heterosexuals with respect to crucial factors of self-esteem, anxiety, depression, behavioral problems, performance in social arenas (sports, school and friendships), use of psychological counseling, mothers' and teachers' reports of children's hyperactivity, unsociability, emotional difficulty, or conduct difficulty.

Nor does empirical research support the misconception that having a homosexual parent has a deleterious effect on children's *gender identity* (i.e., one's psychological sense of being male or female) development. Studies concerning the children of lesbian mothers have not found any difference from those of heterosexual parents in their patterns of gender identity. As a panel of the American Academy of Pediatrics concluded on the basis of their examination of peer-reviewed studies, "[n]one of the more than 300 children studied to date have shown evidence of gender identity confusion, wished to be the other sex, or consistently engaged in cross-gender behavior."

Lesbian and gay parents are as likely as heterosexual parents to provide supportive and healthy environments for their children.

Similarly, most published studies have not found reliable differences in *social gender role* conformity (i.e., adherence to cultural norms defining feminine and masculine behavior) between the children of lesbian and heterosexual mothers. Data have not been reported on the gender identity development or gender role orientation of the sons and daughters of gay fathers.

Currently, there is no scientific consensus about the specific factors that cause an individual to become heterosexual, homosexual, or bisexual—including possible biological, psychological, or social effects of the parents' sexual orientation. However, the available evidence indicates that the vast majority of lesbian and gay adults were raised by heterosexual parents and the vast majority of children raised by lesbian and gay parents eventually grow up to be heterosexual.

Amici emphasize that the abilities of gay and lesbian persons as parents and the positive outcomes for their children are *not* areas where credible scientific researchers disagree. Thus, after careful scrutiny of decades of research in this area, the American Psychological Association concluded in its recent Resolution on Sexual Orientation, Parents, and Children: "There is *no* scientific evidence that parenting effectiveness is related to parental sexual orientation: Lesbian and gay parents are as likely as heterosexual parents to provide supportive and healthy environments for their children" and that "Research has shown that adjustment, development, and psychological well-being of children is unrelated to parental sexual orientation and that the children of lesbian and gay parents are as likely as those of heterosexual parents to flourish." The National Association of Social Workers has determined that "The most striking feature of the research on lesbian mothers, gay fathers, and their children is the absence of pathological findings. The second most striking feature is how similar the groups of gay and lesbian parents and their children are to heterosexual parents and their children that were included in the studies." Most recently, in adopting an official Position Statement in support of legal recognition of same-sex civil marriage, the American Psychiatric Association observed that "no research has shown that the children raised by lesbians and gay men are less well adjusted than those reared within heterosexual relationships." These statements by the leading associations of experts in this area reflect professional consensus that children raised by lesbian or gay parents do not differ in any important respects from those raised by heterosexual parents. No credible empirical research suggests otherwise.

Marriage Would Benefit Children

Allowing same-sex couples to legally marry will not have any detrimental effect on children raised in heterosexual households, but it will benefit children being raised by same-sex couples in at least three ways. First, those children will benefit from having a clearly defined legal relationship with both of their *de facto* parents, particularly for those families that lack the means or wherewithal to complete a second-parent adoption. Such legal clarity is especially important during times of crisis, ranging from school and medical emergencies involving the child to the incapacity or death of a parent. The death of a parent is a highly stressful occasion for a child and is likely to have important effects on the child's well-being. In those situations, the stable legal bonds afforded by marriage can provide the child with as much continuity as possible in her or his relationship with the surviving parent, and can minimize the likelihood of conflicting or competing claims by non-parents for the child's custody.

Second, children will benefit from the greater stability and security that is likely to characterize their parents' relationship when it is legally recognized through marriage. Children benefit when their parents are financially secure, physically and psychologically healthy, and not subjected to high levels of stress. They also benefit when their parents' relationship is stable and likely to endure. Thus, the children of same-sex couples can be expected to benefit when their parents have the legal right to marry.

There is no scientific basis for distinguishing between same-sex couples and heterosexual couples with respect to the legal rights, obligations, benefits, and burdens conferred by civil marriage.

Children in Same-Sex Households Are Healthier than Their Peers

Nicholas Jackson

Nicholas Jackson is the digital director of Pacific Standard *and was the former digital editorial director at* Outside.

When the Supreme Court struck down the 16-year-old Defense of Marriage Act [DOMA] on [June 26, 2013] as part of a pair of decisions that amount to a major victory for the gay rights movement, they also killed the argument that gay marriage is bad for children.

DOMA supporters have long claimed that kids are far better off when they have both a mother and a father at home. (They even go so far as to quote from a 2008 speech by President [Barack] Obama, who supports same-sex marriage, in which he emphasized the role of fathers; "Of all the rocks upon which we build our lives, we are reminded today that family is the most important. And we are called to recognize and honor how critical every father is to that foundation," he said.) Just last week [June 2013], Representative Phil Gingrey (R-Ga.), the leading Republican candidate for a Senate seat in Georgia, told House colleagues on the floor that children would be better off if they were required to take classes on traditional gender roles.

"You know, maybe part of the problem is we need to go back into the schools at a very early age, maybe at the grade school level, and have a class for the young girls and have a class for the young boys and say, you know, this is what's important," he said. Speaking in defense of DOMA ahead of the

Supreme Court decisions, Gingrey noted that, while he understands that the "father knows best" adage is dated, he still believes in it.

But Gingrey is not alone in subscribing to ideas from "back in the old days of television," as he puts it. The argument that the children of same-sex couples are negatively influenced by the family structures in which they are raised came up multiple times during the oral arguments for this case. This, from an amicus brief of "social science professors" submitted to the Supreme Court: "With so many significant outstanding questions about whether children develop as well in same-sex households as in opposite-sex households, it remains prudent for government to continue to recognize marriage as a union of a man and a woman, thereby promoting what is known to be an ideal environment for raising children."

Imaginary Differences of Opinion

As noted in a piece for *The Atlantic* by Philip N. Cohen, a sociologist at the University of Maryland-College Park (and sometimes contributor to *Pacific Standard* partner site *Sociological Images*), [Supreme Court] Justice Antonin Scalia returned to the 40-plus-page brief later: "[T]here's considerable disagreement among sociologists as to what the consequences of raising a child in a single-sex family, whether that is harmful to the child or not," he said.

Being gay is just as healthy as being straight. . . . That goes for the children of same-sex parents too.

Scalia would go on, along with Justice Samuel Alito, to write a dissent to today's court ruling, and even read it from the bench, "a step justices take in a small share of cases, typically to show that they have especially strong views," *The New York Times* reported.

Scalia might have especially strong views, but that doesn't mean they're right. Or even that they have support.

The problem? That brief was found to be based on severely flawed studies. Over at his *Family Inequality* blog, Cohen runs through all of the evidence. It's a fascinating story, as Cohen puts it, "of how Christian conservatives used big private money to produce knowledge in service of their political goals."

In fact, there isn't considerable disagreement among sociologists. As we note in the Five Studies column from our current July/August issue, this one on how we have thought about homosexuality over the past 150 years, "by now virtually all of the major psychiatric, psychological, sociological, and pediatric professional organizations have officially declared that 'being gay is just as healthy as being straight,' as the American Psychological Association puts it. That goes for the children of same-sex parents too."

Also cited in amicus briefs put before the Supreme Court earlier this year was a meta-analysis by Cambridge University psychologist Michael Lamb of more than 100 studies over the last three decades. Lamb's research concluded that "the children and adolescents of same-sex parents are as emotionally healthy, and as educationally and socially successful, as children and adolescents raised by heterosexual parents." It was likely this research to which Kennedy was referring when he wrote, in today's majority opinion (5-4), that DOMA "places same-sex couples in an unstable position of being in a second tier marriage. The differentiation demeans the couple, whose moral and sexual choices the Constitution protects, and whose relationship the state has sought to dignify. And it humiliates tens of thousands of children now being raised by same-sex couples."

Well-Adjusted Children

If it wasn't those briefs, then perhaps Kennedy is familiar with the latest sociological research on the subject. While not as comprehensive as Lamb's meta-analysis, a look at 500 children between the ages of one and 17 as part of the Australian Study of Child Health in Same-Sex Familiar found that children with same-sex parents are actually *healthier* than those with opposite-sex parents. "Because of the situation that same-sex familiar find themselves in, they are generally more willing to communicate and approach the issues that any child may face at school, like teasing or bullying," lead researcher Dr. Simon Crouch, a public health doctor and researcher at the University of Melbourne's McCaughey VicHealth Centre, told *The Sydney Morning Herald*. "This fosters openness and means children tend to be more resilient. That would be our hypothesis."

Father knows some things, certainly. But he's not the only one who knows how to raise happy, healthy children.

Same-Sex Marriage Is Not Good for Families and Children

Ryan T. Anderson

Ryan T. Anderson researches and writes about marriage and religious liberty as the William E. Simon Fellow at The Heritage Foundation, a conservative think tank based in Washington, DC. He is also coauthor of the book What is Marriage? Man and Woman: A Defense.

Marriage is society's best way of ensuring the well-being of children. State recognition of marriage protects children ... by encouraging men and women to commit permanently and exclusively to each other and take responsibility for their children.

Laws on marriage work by promoting a true vision of the institution, making sense of marital norms as a coherent whole. Law affects culture. Culture affects beliefs. Beliefs affect actions. The law teaches, and it shapes the public understanding of what marriage is and what it demands of spouses.

But redefining marriage further distances marriage from the needs of children and denies the importance of mothers and fathers. Redefining marriage rejects as a matter of policy the ideal that children need a mother and a father.

The statistics on the importance of marriage penetrate American life to the extent that President [Barack] Obama can refer to them as well known:

"We know the statistics—that children who grow up without a father are five times more likely to live in poverty and commit crime; nine times more likely to drop out of schools and twenty times more likely to end up in prison," Obama said less than five months before he was elected president in 2008.

"They are more likely to have behavioral problems, or run away from home, or become teenage parents themselves. And the foundations of our community are weaker because of it," he added.

Redefining Marriage

But how can the law teach that fathers are essential if it redefines marriage to make fathers optional? Redefining marriage diminishes the social pressures for husbands to remain with their wives and children, and for men and women to marry before having children.

Redefining marriage to include same-sex relationships makes marriage primarily about emotional union, more about adults' desires than children's needs.

If that's how we understand marriage, marital norms make no sense as a matter of principle. Why require an emotional union to be permanent? Or limited to two persons? Or sexually exclusive (as opposed to "open")?

Weakening marital norms and severing the connection of marriage from responsible procreation are admitted goals of the University of Calgary's Elizabeth Brake and other prominent advocates of redefining marriage.

If justice demands redefining marriage to include the same-sex couple, how long before the courts demand redefining marriage to include throuples and quartets?

Judith Stacey, a professor at NYU, has expressed hope that redefining marriage would give marriage "varied, creative and adaptive contours," leading some to "question the dyadic limitations of Western marriage and seek . . . small group marriages."

More than 300 "LGBT and allied" scholars and advocates called in the statement "Beyond Same-Sex Marriage" for legally recognizing sexual relationships involving more than two partners.

In 2009, *Newsweek* reported that the United States already had over 500,000 polyamorous households. A 2012 article in *New York Magazine* introduced Americans to "throuple," a new term akin to "couple" but with three people.

Indeed, if justice demands redefining marriage to include the same-sex couple, how long before the courts demand redefining marriage to include throuples and quartets?

Weakening the Institution

Some advocates of redefining marriage embrace the goal of weakening the institution of marriage in these very terms. Former President George W. Bush "is correct," writes Victoria Brownworth, "when he states that allowing same-sex couples to marry will weaken the institution of marriage. . . . It most certainly will do so, and that will make marriage a far better concept than it previously has been."

It is no surprise that we see evidence of this occurring. A federal judge in Utah allowed a legal challenge to anti-bigamy laws. A bill allowing a child to have three legal parents last year passed both houses of the California state legislature.

If the law teaches a lie about marriage, it shouldn't surprise us when the consequences of that lie turn out to be bad—for children and society as a whole.

Children Pay a Lifelong Emotional Price for Same-Sex Parenting

Robert Oscar Lopez

Robert Oscar Lopez is the author of a book of gay fiction, Johnson Park, *and editor of the website* English Manif: A Franco-American Flashpoint on Gay Rights Debates. *He is launching an organization called Children's Rights and Ethical Family Alternatives, a new project to discuss the ethics of LGBT family building.*

During oral arguments on [California's same-sex marriage ban initiative] Prop 8, [US Supreme Court] Justice [Anthony] Kennedy alluded to the views of children of same-sex couples as if their desires and concerns are identical to and uncritical of their parents' decisions. But the reality is far more complicated.

During the oral arguments about Proposition 8, Justice Kennedy referred to children being raised by same-sex couples. Since I was one of those children—from ages 2–19, I was raised by a lesbian mother with the help of her partner—I was curious to see what he would say.

I also eagerly anticipated what he would say because I had taken great professional and social risk to file an amicus brief with Doug Mainwaring (who is gay and opposes gay marriage), in which we explained that children deeply feel the loss of a father or mother, no matter how much we love our gay parents or how much they love us. Children feel the loss keenly because they are powerless to stop the decision to deprive them of a father or mother, and the absence of a male or female parent will likely be irreversible for them.

Over the last year I've been in frequent contact with adults who were raised by parents in same-sex partnerships. They are terrified of speaking publicly about their feelings, so several have asked me (since I am already out of the closet, so to speak) to give voice to their concerns.

I cannot speak for *all* children of same-sex couples, but I speak for quite a few of them, especially those who have been brushed aside in the so-called "social science research" on same-sex parenting.

Those who contacted me all professed gratitude and love for the people who raised them, which is why it is so difficult for them to express their reservations about same-sex parenting publicly.

I have always resisted the idea that government should encourage same-sex couples to imagine that their partnerships are indistinguishable from actual marriages. Such a self-definition for gays would be based on a lie.

Emotional Hardships and Conflicting Feelings

Still, they described emotional hardships that came from lacking a mom or a dad. To give a few examples: they feel disconnected from the gender cues of people around them, feel intermittent anger at their "parents" for having deprived them of one biological parent (or, in some cases, both biological parents), wish they had had a role model of the opposite sex, and feel shame or guilt for resenting their loving parents for forcing them into a lifelong situation lacking a parent of one sex.

I have heard of the supposed "consensus" on the soundness of same-sex parenting from pediatricians and psychologists, but that consensus is frankly bogus.

Pediatricians are supposed to make sure kids don't get ringworm or skip out on vaccinations—nobody I know doubts that same-sex couples are able to tend to such basic childcare needs.

Psychologists come from the same field that used to have a "consensus" that homosexuality was a mental disorder. Neither field is equipped to answer the deeper existential dilemmas of legally removing fatherhood or motherhood as a human principle, which is what total "marriage equality" would entail.

I support same-sex civil unions and foster care, but I have always resisted the idea that government should encourage same-sex couples to imagine that their partnerships are indistinguishable from actual marriages. Such a self-definition for gays would be based on a lie, and anything based on a lie will backfire.

The richest and most successful same-sex couple still cannot provide a child something that the poorest and most struggling spouses can provide: a mom and a dad. Having spent forty years immersed in the gay community, I have seen how that reality triggers anger and vicious recrimination from same-sex couples, who are often tempted to bad-mouth so-called "dysfunctional" or "trashy" straight couples in order to say, "We deserve to have kids more than they do!"

No Substitute for a Mom and a Dad

But I am here to say no, having a mom and a dad is a precious value in its own right and not something that can be overridden, even if a gay couple has lots of money, can send a kid to the best schools, and raises the kid to be an Eagle Scout.

It's disturbingly classist and elitist for gay men to think they can love their children unreservedly after treating their surrogate mother like an incubator, or for lesbians to think they can love their children unconditionally after treating their sperm-donor father like a tube of toothpaste.

It's also racist and condescending for same-sex couples to think they can strong-arm adoption centers into giving them orphans by wielding financial or political clout. An orphan in Asia or in an American inner city has been entrusted to adoption authorities to make the best decision for the child's life, not to meet a market demand for same-sex couples wanting children. (Whatever trauma caused them to be orphans shouldn't be compounded with the stress of being adopted into a same-sex partnership.)

Lastly, it's harmful to everyone if gay men and lesbians in mixed-orientation marriages with children file for divorce so they can enter same-sex couplings and raise their children with a new homosexual partner while kicking aside the other biological parent. Kids generally want their mom and dad to stop fighting, put aside their differences, and stay together, even if one of them is gay.

The fact is that same-sex parenting suffers from insurmountable logistical problems for which children pay the steepest lifelong price.

In my family's case, my mother was divorced and she made the best decision given our circumstances. Had she set out to create a same-sex parenting family in a premeditated fashion, I would probably not feel at peace with her memory, because I would know that my lack of a strong father figure during childhood did not result from an accident of life history, but rather from her own careless desire to have her cake and eat it too. I am blessed not to contend with such a traumatic thought about my own mother. I love her because I know she did everything possible to give me a good life. Still, what was best in our specific circumstances was a state of deprivation that it is unconscionable to force on innocent children if it's not absolutely necessary.

Justice Kennedy alluded to the views of children being raised by same-sex couples as if our desires and concerns are identical to and uncritical of the decisions made by our parents. The reality is far more complicated than that.

Children Pay the Price

Putting aside all the historical analogies to civil rights and the sentimental platitudes about love, the fact is that same-sex parenting suffers from insurmountable logistical problems for which children pay the steepest lifelong price.

Whether it's by surrogacy, insemination, divorce, or commercialized adoption, moral hazards abound for same-sex couples who insist on replicating a heterosexual model of parenthood. The children thrown into the middle of these moral hazards are well aware of their parents' role in creating a stressful and emotionally complicated life for kids, which alienates them from cultural traditions like Father's Day and Mother's Day, and places them in the unenviable position of being called "homophobes" if they simply suffer the natural stress that their parents foisted on them—and admit to it.

Same-sex marriage would pose no problems for me if it were simply about couples being together. As a bisexual I get that. But unfortunately the LGBT movement decided that its validation by others requires a redefinition of "marriage" to include same-sex partnerships. So here we are, stuck having to encourage problematic lives for children in order to affirm same-sex couples the way the movement demands.

That's why I am for civil unions but not for redefining marriage. But I suppose I don't count—I am no doctor, judge, or television commentator, just a kid who had to clean up the mess left behind by the sexual revolution.

Gay Marriage, Then Group Marriage?

Robert P. George, Sherif Girgis, and Ryan T. Anderson

Robert P. George, Sherif Girgis, and Ryan T. Anderson are coauthors of the book What Is Marriage? Man and Woman: A Defense.

The attractive civil rights rhetoric of "marriage equality" masks a profound error about what marriage is.

Of course, if marriage were simply about recognizing bonds of affection or romance, then two men or two women could form a marriage just as a man and woman can. But so could three or more in the increasingly common phenomenon of group ("polyamorous") partnerships. In that case, to recognize opposite-sex unions but not same-sex or polyamorous ones would be unfair—a denial of equality.

But marriage is far more than your emotional bond with "your Number One person," to quote same-sex marriage proponent John Corvino. Just as the act that makes marital love also makes new life, so marriage itself is a multilevel—bodily as well as emotional—union that would be fulfilled by procreation and family life. That is what justifies its distinctive norms—monogamy, exclusivity, permanence—and the concept of marital consummation by conjugal intercourse.

It is also what explains and justifies the government's involvement in marriage.

The government takes no notice of companionship for its own sake, romantic or otherwise. But it has powerful reasons to ensure that whenever possible, children have the benefit of being reared by the mom and dad whose union gave them life.

Equality Argument Could Extend to Plural Marriages

All human beings are equal in dignity and should be equal before the law. But equality only forbids arbitrary distinctions. And there is nothing arbitrary about maximizing the chances that children will know the love of their biological parents in a committed and exclusive bond. A strong marriage culture serves children, families and society by encouraging the ideal of giving kids both a mom and a dad.

Indeed, if that is not the public purpose of marriage law, then the "injustice" and "bigotry" charges comes back to bite most same-sex marriage supporters.

If marriage is just the emotional bond "that matters most" to you—in the revealing words of the circuit judge who struck down California Proposition 8—then personal tastes or a couple's subjective preferences aside, there is no reason of principle for marriage to be pledged to permanence. Or sexually exclusive rather than "open." Or limited to two spouses. Or oriented to family life and shaped by its demands.

> *In the manifesto "Beyond Same-Sex Marriage," 300 leading "LGBT and allied" scholars and activists call for the recognition of multiple partner relationships.*

In that case, every argument for recognizing two men's bond as marital—equality, destigmatization, extending economic benefits—would also apply to recognizing romantic triads ("throuples," as they are now known). Refusing such recognition would be unfair—a violation of equality—if commitment based on emotional companionship is what makes a marriage.

But don't take our word for it. Many prominent leaders of the campaign to redefine marriage make precisely the same point. (We provide many more examples, and full citations, in the amicus brief we filed with the Supreme Court on the harms of redefining marriage.)

What Same-Sex Marriage Advocates Say

University of Calgary Professor Elizabeth Brake supports "minimal marriage," in which people distribute whichever duties they choose, among however many partners, of whatever sex.

NYU [New York University] Professor Judith Stacey hopes that redefining marriage would give marriage "varied, creative, and adaptive contours . . ." and lead to acceptance of "small group marriages." In the manifesto "Beyond Same-Sex Marriage," 300 leading "LGBT and allied" scholars and activists call for the recognition of multiple partner relationships.

Influential columnist and "It Gets Better" founder Dan Savage encourages spouses to adopt "a more flexible attitude" about sex outside their marriage. Journalist Victoria Brownworth cheerfully predicts that same-sex marriage will "weaken the institution of marriage."

"It most certainly will do so," she says, "and that will make marriage a far better concept than it previously has been."

Author Michelangelo Signorile urges same-sex partners to "demand the right to marry not as a way of adhering to society's moral codes but rather to debunk a myth and radically alter an archaic institution." They should "fight for same-sex marriage and its benefits and then, once granted, redefine the institution of marriage completely, because the most subversive action lesbians and gay men can undertake . . . is to transform the notion of 'family' entirely."

These leading same-sex marriage advocates are correct.

Redefining marriage would, by further eroding its central norms, weaken an institution that has already been battered by widespread divorce, out-of-wedlock child bearing and the like.

People who think that would be good for children, families and society generally should support "marriage equality." People who believe otherwise shouldn't be taken in by the deceptive rhetoric.

CHAPTER 4

What Are Some Other Key Issues with Same-Sex Marriage?

Chapter Preface

While the state-by-state legalization or prohibition of same-sex marriage is creating a nationwide patchwork of laws for recognizing such unions or expressly prohibiting them, it is also creating an equally confusing tapestry of conditions for formally ending those legal relationships. Consequently, many same-sex couples are discovering that the right to get married does not necessarily include the right to get divorced—a situation known in the LGBT community as being "wed-locked."

As the number of states legalizing same-sex marriage grows, dozens of nonmarriage states still refuse to recognize same-sex marriages performed elsewhere, even for the purpose of legally dissolving them. The basis for that refusal is that granting same-sex divorce in effect acknowledges the validity of the marriage, a precedent that could lead to overturning a state's same-sex marriage ban.

Even though the federal government now recognizes same-sex marriages performed in any state, same-sex couples who move to marriage-prohibiting states after getting married elsewhere face formidable obstacles if they decide to divorce, as do residents of nonrecognition states who marry outside their home state.

According to a study by M.V. Lee Badgett and Jody L. Herman for the Williams Institute, an LGBT legal think tank, "when a state allows marriage for same-sex couples, couples will travel to that state to marry from nearby states and from large states in which they do not enjoy that same opportunity."[1]

---

1. M.V. Lee Badgett and Jody L. Herman, "Patterns of Relationship Recognition by Same-Sex Couples in the United States," Williams Institute, November 2011. http://williamsinstitute.law.ucla.edu/wp-content/uploads/Badgett-Herman-Marriage-Dissolution-Nov-2011.pdf.

For such couples that later split up, the remedy is not as simple as revisiting the state where they were married to get a divorce. Most states have residency requirements of six months to a year for both parties in order to grant a divorce, and some have even stricter regulations that require marriage counseling, periods of physical separation, sexual abstinence between the married individuals, or long waiting periods before a court will finalize divorce papers.

But even in states where same-sex marriage is now legal, divorce can be a long, drawn-out process because courts are grappling with all sorts of new issues, such as navigating outdated legal statutes that refer to the divorcing parties as "husband" and "wife," or figuring out how to divide assets based on the true length of the partnership of longtime couples who only recently obtained the right to marry. And if the divorcing couple has children, the complications can multiply exponentially.

When a straight couple with children divorces, a judge typically determines custody rights, visitation, and child support based on the child's best interest. But for same-sex couples, the issue of parental rights can be even more complicated and heartbreaking, especially if the state considers only one partner a legal parent. Many states—even some that do permit same-sex marriages—do not recognize "de facto" parents, those who "share (at least) equally in primary childcare responsibilities while residing with a child for reasons other than money," according to the American Law Institute's definition.

According to the Williams Institute, although a smaller percentage of same-sex couples marry compared to straight couples, if current trends continue the marriage rates will be similar in about ten years. And while married same-sex couples currently dissolve their marriages slightly less frequently than straight couples do, half of all heterosexual marriages do eventually end in divorce. The expectation is that as states expand marriage rights and more same-sex couples wed, there will be an increasing demand for divorce equality to accompany marriage equality.

For now, however, the laws and regulations governing same-sex divorce and the dissolution of same-sex domestic partnerships are in flux and the conditions continue to evolve along with the marriage landscape itself. The need for legal clarity on same-sex divorce is just one of the side effects of legalizing same-sex marriage. The authors in this chapter discuss a variety of other topics—religious, social, and economic—related to the newly acquired and still-expanding marriage rights of same-sex couples.

Same-Sex Marriage Has Negative Consequences for Religious Liberty

Institute for Marriage and Public Policy

The Institute for Marriage and Public Policy is a nonprofit, non-partisan organization dedicated to research and education on ways that law and public policy can strengthen marriage as a social institution.

The experiences of many jurisdictions demonstrate that redefining marriage to include same-sex couples will create conflict with the free exercise of religion for those who believe marriage is the legal union of one man and one woman as husband and wife. The instances that follow provide a picture of the kinds of areas in which these conflicts may occur. Some of these items have not yet occurred in states in which marriage has been redefined, but the likelihood of each example dramatically increases when the government begins to view opposition to same-sex marriage as a prohibited form of discrimination.

Adoption and Foster Care Agencies

District of Columbia. At the beginning of 2010, the Catholic Archdiocese of Washington, D.C. ceased its foster care placement program because, given the District's new same-sex marriage law, it would no longer have been permitted to limit its placement of children to the homes of married heterosexual couples.

Illinois. In Illinois, gay rights groups are arguing that Catholic Charities and two other religious adoption agencies are ineligible for public funds, [and] a formal investigation into discrimination has been launched, and the Attorney General's office and Department of Child and Family Services are now considering whether existing anti-discrimination provisions would prohibit religious agencies that do not place children with same-sex couples from participating on an equal basis with other adoption agencies. Because of the expensive potential threat of litigation, Rockford Catholic Charities has already decided to close, absent specific religious liberty protection.

Massachusetts. In the wake of the *Goodridge v. Department of Public Health* decision, Massachusetts Catholic Charities sought an exemption from State law requiring adoption agencies to make no distinctions on the basis of sexual orientation. Catholic Charities could not do so without violating its religious mandate. The legislature refused the exemption, and Catholic Charities had to withdraw from the adoption business. Any possible relief from the judiciary was clearly not feasible because of the *Goodridge* court's equation of parenting by same-sex couples and married couples.

New York. Adoption.com, an online adoption service, only provides adoptive parent profiles for married couples, so both California and New York have barred it from doing business in those states.

A Mississippi counselor was fired for refusing to provide relationship counseling to unmarried couples.

Churches and Related Facilities

New Jersey. The Methodist Ocean Grove Camp Meeting Association in New Jersey, which, as required by church law, declined to allow its property to be used for a civil union ceremony, was sued for discrimination. The lawsuit was supported by the attorney general's office and resulted in an Association decision to cease allowing the property to be used for weddings.

Counselors

Georgia. A contract counselor with the Centers for Disease Control referred an employee in a same-sex relationship to another counselor because of the first counselor's religious objection to facilitating a same-sex relationship. Although the second counselor was satisfactory, the employee "felt 'judged and condemned'" and felt "that plaintiff's nonverbal communication also indicated disapproval of her relationship." After investigating the complaint, plaintiff was laid off. She sued, alleging (1) a violation of free exercise, (2) a violation of the Religious Freedom Restoration Act, and (3) a violation of Title VII's prohibition of religious discrimination. The court said that because the CDC was acting as an employer, the standard of review is more deferential to its decision. Here, the court said "there is no evidence in the record to suggest that the CDC removed plaintiff from the contract because of her religiously based need to refer clients seeking same-sex relationship counseling"; rather "the CDC removed plaintiff from the contract because of the manner in which plaintiff handled the situation involving [client], and the CDC's reasonable concern about how plaintiff would handle similar situations in the future." Thus, the firing created no substantial burden on the plaintiff's free exercise of religion. Since the CDC's decision was "not based upon plaintiff's religiously based refusal to provide same-sex relationship counseling" but on "the manner in which plaintiff handled the situation," there was no RFRA violation. For the same reason, the Title VII claim failed. Additionally, the employer's offer of employment reassignment services was considered a reasonable accommodation of the plaintiff's religious objection.

Maine. A licensed school guidance counselor was the subject of a complaint seeking to have his license revoked after he appeared in a television commercial in favor of a ballot referendum to restore the definition of marriage in Maine to the union of a man and a woman.

Mississippi. A Mississippi counselor was fired for refusing to provide relationship counseling to unmarried couples. The counselor's Title VII claim was denied after the court found that the accommodation of the employee's religious beliefs would have worked an undue burden on the employer.

Dating Service

New Jersey. A homosexual man sued an online dating service because it did not offer an option for men seeking to date other men. The Division on Civil Rights of the New Jersey Attorney General's Office intervened in the lawsuit on the side of the plaintiff and the company opted to settle, agreeing to change the options on its site and to pay $5,000 to the plaintiff and $50,000 to the Division.

Employment

District of Columbia. After the District redefined marriage to include same-sex couples, the Archdiocese of Washington, D.C. was forced to change its health coverage for employees so as to avoid discrimination claims for not offering benefits to employees' same-sex partners.

> *When New York changed its law to allow same-sex couples to marry, at least two clerks have resigned rather than sign marriage licenses for same-sex couples, and others may be required to do so.*

California. A consultant for Cisco Systems was fired by the company after a manager at the company learned he had once written a book opposing same-sex marriage.

Government Officials

Massachusetts. After the Supreme Judicial Court required the state to issue marriage licenses to same-sex couples, the governor's chief legal counsel told Justices of the Peace in the state that they must "follow the law, whether you like it or not." State officials announced that "Justices of the Peace who refuse to perform gay weddings will be asked to resign and could face formal discrimination charges if they don't." As a result, some Justices of the Peace expressed their intention to resign rather than perform same-sex marriages.

Iowa. After the Iowa Supreme Court mandated same-sex marriage, the attorney general wrote to county recorders and told them they must issue marriage licenses to same-sex couples and warned: "if necessary, we will explore legal actions to enforce and implement the Court's ruling, working with the Iowa Dept. of Public Health and county attorneys." As a result, at least one Iowa magistrate no longer performs weddings.

New York. When New York changed its law to allow same-sex couples to marry, at least two clerks have resigned rather than sign marriage licenses for same-sex couples, and others may be required to do so. The Nassau County District Attorney threatened clerks who decline to participate in same-sex marriages with criminal prosecution. Governor Andrew Cuomo responded to the first resignation by saying: "if you can't enforce the law, then you shouldn't be in that position."

Harassment

New Jersey. A bridal salon owner who told a customer seeking a dress for a same-sex union ceremony that same-sex marriage was not "right" was subjected to a campaign of vilification on a business rating site despite the site's policy that postings were only to be made by individuals who had actually patronized the business.

Married Student Housing

New York. In 2001, the New York Court of Appeals ruled that Yeshiva University's married student housing policy violated the New York City Human Rights Law prohibiting discrimination on the basis of sexual orientation. The Yeshiva University College of Medicine housing policy limited residence to medical students, their spouses and children, while also giving married couples priority over unmarried students in certain situations. Plaintiffs in the case had been denied the opportunity to live with their unmarried (non-student) partner in on-campus housing.

Medical Professionals

California. Shortly after the California Supreme Court redefined marriage, the court heard a case involving a doctor who had referred a woman in a same-sex couple to another doctor for artificial insemination because of his religious concerns about participating in the procedure. The court held that the doctor could claim no religious exemption to the civil rights law under which he was sued because of the State's overwhelming interest in ending sexual orientation discrimination, a policy one judge identified as emanating from the court's marriage decision.

> *The Methodist Ocean Grove Camp Meeting Association in New Jersey, which . . . declined to allow its property to be used for a civil union ceremony, was stripped of a tax benefit given to property owners who allow public access to the beach.*

Parents

Massachusetts. In a recent case, parents of young elementary school students objected to curriculum and classroom discussions meant to inculcate in the children the idea that there are no differences between the marriages of husbands and wives and those involving same-sex couples. A panel of the U.S. Court of Appeals for the First Circuit held that public schools "have an interest in promoting tolerance, including for the children (and parents) of gay marriages."

Private Club

Iowa. After the Des Moines Human Rights Commission ruled that defining "family" (for membership enrollment purposes) to include only married couples was likely sexual orientation discrimination, the YMCA changed its policy to allow unmarried couples to purchase family memberships.

Social Services

Maine. As a condition of access to city housing and community redevelopment funds, a religious charity was required to extend employee spousal benefit programs to registered same-sex couples.

Tax Exemption

New Jersey. The Methodist Ocean Grove Camp Meeting Association in New Jersey, which, as required by church law, declined to allow its property to be used for a civil union ceremony, was stripped of a tax benefit given to property owners who allow public access to the beach.

Teachers and Students

Florida. A social studies teacher was removed from his classroom after he posted a comment on Facebook critical of same-sex marriage.

Missouri. A social work student was accused of violating her school's code of conduct when, for reasons of her faith, she refused to sign a letter to the State Legislature advocating adoptions by same-sex couples. After she filed suit, the university quickly settled and took corrective action to clear the student's name and make other restitution.

Michigan. A graduate student at Eastern Michigan University was dismissed from the school's counseling program after asking for permission to refer a client to another counselor because she was uncomfortable affirming the same-sex relationship of the client.

Wedding-Related Professional Services

Illinois. The owners of two bed and breakfasts were sued by a same-sex couple. The couple also filed complaints with the attorney general's office, which is investigating whether the owners' decision to use their facilities only for weddings is unlawful discrimination.

New Mexico. A wedding photographer was successfully sued for declining to photograph a same-sex commitment ceremony. The New Mexico Human Rights Commission ruled in favor of the complainant and levied a nearly $7,000 fine against the photographer. The New Mexico Court of Appeals affirmed that decision.

A psychotherapist [in England] has been threatened with the loss of her professional license after she agreed to help a man who came to her claiming to want help with unwanted same-sex attraction.

Vermont. The ACLU [American Civil Liberties Union] sued the owners of the Wildflower Inn in Vermont because the owners [of the inn], based on their Catholic faith, declined to host a wedding reception for a same-sex couple from New York. The Inn agreed to settle the lawsuit for $30,000.

International Adoption and Foster Care Agencies

England. After U.K. law required adoption agencies to comply with sexual orientation discrimination provisions, a Catholic agency sought to amend its Charter to specify that it would offer its services only to opposite-sex couples in order to take advantage of a statutory exception for organizations whose purpose was to serve a specific population. The Charities Commission would not allow the amendment. The High Court reversed the decision and ordered the Commission to reconsider because the court believed the relevant statutory language allowed the kind of amendment the charity sought and that the agency could provide a bona fide public benefit to the population it primarily served—hard to place children—even if it did not place children with same-sex couples.

International Churches and Related Facilities

Canada. Two women, Deborah Chymyshyn and Tracey Smith, filed a complaint with the British Columbia Human Rights Tribunal against the Knights of Columbus in response to the Knight's decision to terminate the couple's facility rental agreement after the Knights learned that the banquet hall was to be used for a same-sex wedding. . . .

International Counselors

England. A psychotherapist has been threatened with the loss of her professional license after she agreed to help a man who came to her claiming to want help with unwanted same-sex attraction. The feigned client was seeking to entrap the therapist.

England. A relationship counselor declined to participate in "psycho-sexual therapy" with same-sex couples and was fired. The court said it was bound by an earlier decision which held that there was no discrimination where an employee was fired for refusing to participate in civil partnership ceremonies because of her religious beliefs. The court also disavowed a submission from the former Archbishop of Canterbury, in which he argued that English law offers "vigorous protection of the Christian's right (and every other person's right) to hold and express his or her beliefs," stating that the court should not "offer any protection whatever of the substance or content of those beliefs on the ground only that they are based on religious precepts."

International Employment

Canada. A sportscaster who made a comment on Twitter favoring marriage as the union of a man and a woman as husband and wife, in response to a hockey player's comment favoring same-sex marriage, was fired by his employer.

The Archdiocese of Liverpool has claimed that, due to legal restrictions, it cannot fire a Catholic headmaster who is in a same-sex civil partnerships.

Canada. An evangelical charity that operates residential homes for people with disabilities fired a lesbian employee. In a subsequent lawsuit, the court ordered the ministry to adopt a nondiscrimination policy regarding sexual orientation and train its employees not to discriminate on that basis.

England. The Cardiff Employment Tribunal ruled that an Anglican Bishop's refusal to hire a gay youth minister was sexual orientation discrimination.

England. The Archdiocese of Liverpool has claimed that, due to legal restrictions, it cannot fire a Catholic headmaster who is in a same-sex civil partnerships.

International Foster Parents

England. A Christian couple sought to be foster parents, but the Foster Panel did not proceed with their application because the potential parents' views, in the words of an assessor, "did not equate with the Fostering Standards where they related to the need to value diversity, address a child's needs in relation to their sexuality, enhance the child's feeling of self-worth and help the child to deal with all forms of discrimination." . . .

Canada. A decision of the Canadian Broadcast Standards Council found a Canadian radio station had violated the Canadian Association of Broadcasters' *Code of Ethics* in broadcasting a segment of the February 9, 1997 Focus on the Family radio program dealing with homosexuality.

Canada. Although subsequently dropped, Catholic Bishop Fred Henry was the subject of complaints to the Alberta Human Rights Commission for a pastoral letter opposing same-sex marriage.

Christopher Kempling, a secondary teacher in the Quesnel School District [in Canada], was cited for professional misconduct in connection with an article and several letters to the editor, all critical of homosexual behavior.

International Government Officials

Canada. After Canada redefined marriage, marriage commissioners in a number of provinces resigned rather than perform the marriages. A marriage commissioner in Saskatchewan refused to perform a same-sex marriage ceremony because of religious objections. . . . The court found nothing in Canadian law that would provide a religious exemption from the responsibility not to discriminate in performing marriages. The court found that the commissioner acting on his religious beliefs "constitutes discrimination in the provision of a public service on the basis of sexual orientation."

England. An Islington registrar alleged religious discrimination when she was threatened with firing for refusing to perform civil partnerships. She objected on religious grounds and had been informally accommodated until two fellow employees complained. . . . The court concluded that the registrar's "proper and genuine desire to have her religious views relating to marriage respected should not be permitted to override Islington's concern to ensure that all its registrars manifest equal respect for the homosexual community as for the heterosexual community."

Netherlands. Marriage commissioners in the Netherlands are required to perform same-sex marriages, and a district of Amsterdam has begun requiring annual examinations to ensure commissioners there are willing to participate in the ceremonies.

International Religious Schools

Canada. A private religious college associated with the Evangelical Free Church of Canada was denied accreditation by the British Columbia College of Teachers. The accreditation was denied because the college's code of conduct, which applied to all faculty, staff, and students, prohibited "homosexual behaviour." According to the College of Teachers, "Labelling homosexual behaviour as sinful has the effect of excluding persons whose sexual orientation is gay or lesbian. The Council believes and is supported by law in the belief that sexual orientation is no more separable from a person than colour. Persons of homosexual orientation, like persons of colour, are entitled to protection and freedom from discrimination under the law." The Supreme Court of Canada reversed, holding that while an individual teacher may be sanctioned for discriminatory behavior, "the freedom of individuals to adhere to certain religious beliefs while at TWU should be respected." . . .

International Teachers

Canada. In 2001, Christopher Kempling, a secondary teacher in the Quesnel School District, was cited for professional misconduct in connection with an article and several letters to the editor, all critical of homosexual behavior, which were published in a local newspaper. The Disciplinary Committee of the College of Teachers later found him guilty of conduct unbecoming a member of the British Columbia College of

Teachers and suspended his teaching certificate for one month. This decision was recently upheld against Mr. Kempling's Charter of Rights and Freedoms Challenge by the British Columbia Court of Appeals.

International Wedding-Related Services

Canada. As reported by the Prince Edward Island Human Rights Commission: "In August 2000, a gay couple filed a human rights complaint alleging discrimination in accommodations on the basis of sexual orientation. The couple was visiting the Island and made reservations for two at a local bed and breakfast. When they arrived, the owner refused to rent the two men one room with one bed. The Respondent maintains that she acted in accordance with her belief that two unrelated adults of the same sex should not sleep in the same bed. The parties reached a settlement in March 2001. The Respondent agreed to cease operating a bed and breakfast or any other tourist accommodation and to pay the Complainants a sum of general damages. Furthermore, if the Respondent commenced to operate a tourist facility in the future, they would provide the Commission assurance of compliance with the Human Rights Act."

Canada. Owners of a bed and breakfast in British Columbia shut down their business after having a complaint filed with the provincial Human Rights Tribunal because they declined to accommodate a same-sex couple seeking a shared room.

England. The owners of a private hotel were sued by a same-sex couple when the hotel declined to let them share a room because of the owners' religious objections to unmarried sexual behavior.

Same-Sex Marriage Does Not Impact Religious Freedom

David Lampo

David Lampo is director of publications at the Cato Institute, a libertarian think tank based in Washington, DC.

The opponents of same-sex marriage have thrown out many arguments against it, most of them without a rational basis or designed simply to obscure their real reason for opposition: They simply don't think homosexuals deserve the same legal rights that they do.

These arguments are mostly falling on deaf ears, apparently, since public opinion continues to change in favor of marriage equality, but that doesn't stop opponents from using half truths, misrepresentations, or even outright lies to advance their agenda.

One of their favorite arguments of late is that legalizing same-sex marriage will somehow lead to restrictions on religious liberty, even "criminalization" of religious opposition to homosexuality, and many conservative religious leaders and pundits are now making this argument the centerpiece of their campaign against gay marriage. Politicians that pander to them are speaking out as well, such as Sen. Ted Cruz, the Tea Party Republican from Texas making waves on Capitol Hill for his strident defense of conservative social issues.

He recently told the Christian Broadcasting Network's David Brody, for example, that "other nations that have gone down the road towards gay marriage" are punishing "Christian pastors who decline to perform gay marriages" and who "speak out and preach biblical truths on marriage," warning that could happen here. A scary thought, to be sure, certainly one that seems to merit the concern of every freedom-loving conservative and libertarian in this country.

Except that it's not true.

Cruz and other opponents of same-sex marriage point to the 2003 case of a Swedish Pentecostal minister named Aake Green, who was taken to court for comparing homosexuality to cancer, as the perfect example of the slippery slope gay marriage will put us on. His 2004 conviction, however, had nothing to do with gay marriage, which didn't even exist at the time. Aake was charged under Sweden's hate crimes statute. Unlike America, many European countries lack the free speech guarantees we take for granted. Even in Sweden, however, his conviction was ultimately overturned. Apparently, facts rarely get in the way of a politician or a preacher on a mission.

None of the states in which these cases were heard even had same-sex marriage at the time of their respective lawsuits.

A Same-Sex Marriage Bait and Switch

The same is true here in the United States. Opponents of same sex marriage cannot point to a single case where a church or religious institution in America has been forced to conduct or sanction a same sex wedding. In fact, those states that have adopted same-sex marriage have instituted strict protections for the right of churches to refuse to recognize or support such marriages, consistent with our heritage of freedom of religion and conscience. So instead, the opponents of gay marriage are engaged in an intellectual bait and switch argument, trying to tie gay marriage laws to a variety of lawsuits against private businesses for discrimination against gay couples.

Conservative columnist Dana Loesch has been particularly outspoken at this game, citing a number of such cases that she says prove that same-sex marriage will put us on that slippery slope to the day when opponents of gay rights and same-sex marriage will have their religious rights and freedom of conscience routinely violated:

- In 2006, a Christian photographer in New Mexico turned down a request by a gay couple to shoot their wedding photos, and she was then sued for her refusal to do so. The state's Human Rights Commission ruled in favor of the couple, as did the New Mexico Court of Appeals. The case is now before the state supreme court.

- In New Jersey, a Methodist church received a property tax exemption by promising to make its grounds open to the public, and it received taxpayer support for upkeep of the property as well. But when a lesbian couple tried to rent a pavilion on the property for a civil union ceremony (New Jersey doesn't have gay marriage), the church turned them down. The state then revoked the tax exemption it had granted.

- In Lexington, Kentucky, a T-shirt company called Hands On Originals refused to print shirts for the local Gay and Lesbian Services Organization based on the company's religious beliefs. The group sued, and the company was dragged through a lengthy legal investigation by the county Human Rights Commission. The case now goes to a public hearing for resolution.

- A Colorado bakery was sued by a gay couple last year after the firm refused to bake them a wedding cake. The case is scheduled to be heard before the state's Civil Rights Commission in September. If the bakery loses and refuses to comply with the order, the owner could face a fine of $500 and up to a year in jail.

- Two years ago in Montpelier, Vermont, the Wildflower Inn refused to host a wedding reception for a lesbian couple from New York, saying that hosting such an event would violate their religious views. The couple sued with the help of the ACLU, and last year reached an agreement with the inn that forced it to stop holding wedding receptions and fined it $30,000.

As upsetting as these cases are for anyone who believes in freedom of association and religion, the simple fact is that none of them had anything to do with legalizing same-sex marriage, as so many conservatives like to argue.

The opponents of same-sex marriage are losing the battle for Americans' hearts and minds, and their dishonesty will make their defeat even sweeter for those who believe in legal equality for all Americans.

Lawsuits Were Not About Marriage

All of these lawsuits were based on the defendants allegedly violating their states' or local governments' respective public accommodations laws, laws that prohibit businesses that cater to the public from discrimination on the basis of sexual orientation (as well as on the basis of a variety of other personal characteristics such as race, creed, religion, sex, and national origin). None of the states in which these cases were heard even had same-sex marriage at the time of their respective lawsuits. . . .

Surely Ms. Loesch and others know that these lawsuits, legally speaking, have nothing to so with same-sex marriage, yet they argue otherwise.

One can certainly make (and in my opinion, *should* make) the argument that all of the defendants in these cases should be free to withhold their services from those they morally disagree with; that, after all is what freedom of association and freedom of religion are all about.

But *lying* about these cases in a cynical attempt to denigrate marriage equality is intellectually and morally dishonest, revealing a growing desperation on the part of the anti-gay marriage movement in this country. The opponents of same-sex marriage are losing the battle for Americans' hearts and minds, and their dishonesty will make their defeat even sweeter for those who believe in legal equality for all Americans.

Beyond Gay Marriage—Is the LGBT Movement Walking down the Aisle to Nowhere?

Kenyon Farrow, Josh Friedes, and Yasmin Nair, interviewed by Rebecca Burns

Kenyon Farrow is the former director of Queers for Economic Justice; Josh Friedes is the director of marriage equality at Equal Rights Washington; Yasmin Nair is a Chicago writer with the radical queer collective Against Equality. Rebecca Burns is the assistant editor at In These Times, *a politically progressive monthly magazine.*

As LGBT pride month rang in this June [2012], the gay rights movement seemed to have much to celebrate. President [Barack] Obama's announcement of support for same-sex marriage, though denounced by some as a contrived political move, was followed by the overturn of part of the Defense of Marriage Act by a federal appeals court. But these apparent wins haven't resolved a longstanding debate within the LGBT community: Is winning the right to marry really a victory? Many queer activists argue that the narrow focus on marriage has eclipsed other issues and tamed a once-radical movement. *In These Times* discussed the direction of LGBT organizing with Kenyon Farrow, former director of Queers for Economic Justice; Josh Friedes, director of marriage equality at Equal Rights Washington; and Yasmin Nair, a Chicago writer with the radical queer collective, Against Equality, who also organizes youth with Gender JUST.

Same-sex marriage is on the ballot in four states this No-vember [2012]. What's the outlook for these initiatives, especially in light of statements of support from President Obama and other leaders?

Josh: The statements from these leaders are huge. They provide a pathway for many people to evolve their positions, and we're seeing public support for equality increasing. I am extremely optimistic that 2012 will be the year where we see the first marriage equality ballot initiative move positively through an electorate.

Yasmin: This may be true, but the notion that marriage is some kind of magic button that, when you press it, makes things better for LGBT people, is a dangerous one because it can be untrue in so many instances. The assumption that marrying will extend healthcare to the family members of LGBT people ignores the fact that many of us cannot access healthcare in the first place. The people who are going to ben-efit the most from gay marriage will be the ones who already have the resources.

Kenyon: And plenty of people are willing to support mar-riage equality who may not support any other aspect of a pro-gressive agenda. The LGBT equality movement is moving fur-ther and further to the right, and now we're developing relationships and even Super PACs with Republican donors who, for personal reasons, are willing to fundraise for mar-riage equality.

Part of this question is about the nature of marriage itself. Does it benefit LGBT people to gain entry to an institution that many consider heteronormative [a world view that promotes heterosexuality as the normal or preferred sexual orientation]?

Josh: If you look at the arc of history—whether it is anti-miscegenation laws or those restricting the rights of Jews to marry—marriage is often used as a way of making people "the other." If LGBT people are going to be seen as fully equal, we need to overcome this.

Kenyon: There's also an equally long history of the state compelling people to marry. The argument in the '90s, that what poor women really needed was to get married, provided cover for the state to abandon large parts of its welfare and food stamp programs. We're also seeing that in states with same-sex marriage, companies are now dumping their domestic partnership benefits, which sometimes were not just for gay couples, but also for unmarried straight couples or family members. So there's actually a way in which marriage becomes not a civil right, but a civil demand from the state in order to get benefits.

If marriage is truly a choice, then the unmarried should be able to receive the same benefits as the married.

Josh: Freedom to marry includes the freedom to reject marriage. But I don't believe in this notion of heteronormativity. I believe that an incredible number of people choose to form a lifelong bond with another person and have that recognized. If marriage had remained a very unequal institution, LGBT people would be working for domestic partnerships or some other status. But marriage has become an increasingly egalitarian institution, and therefore has become more appealing to gay and lesbian people.

Yasmin: The idea that marriage has transformed from a profoundly unequal institution into an equal one is untrue. It has shifted a bit, perhaps: You're not allowed to beat your wife and get away with it these days. But what has definitely not shifted is the state's role in marriage, in using marriage as a pivot to take away benefits. What marriage does is persuade us that it's our sole, private responsibility to take care of our families, and that only through a marriage contract will we be granted lifesaving benefits. If marriage is truly a choice, then the unmarried should be able to receive the same benefits as the married.

And that's not just an anti-assimilationist argument; you're also implicating the push for marriage equality in privatization and austerity.

Kenyon: Yes, politicians are often given a pass on other issues when they come out for marriage equality. People all over the country laud [New York] Mayor [Michael] Bloomberg for his support of same-sex marriage. But in his recent budget, there was a 70 percent cut in homeless youth services, as many as half of whom identify as LGBT. And many of the LGBT equality organizations, after praising these politicians, don't show up to the budget hearings to defend these services.

Do we have to juxtapose marriage rights and economic justice? Could marriage equality be a pathway to winning other rights?

Josh: I think attacks on marriage equality are a bit of red herring. You can look at the budget cuts in New York and blame it on marriage. But you can also look at states without marriage equality and see how much less there is for LGBT people. In Washington state, the political power that has built around the marriage issue has resulted in transgender hate-crime and anti-bullying statutes.

AIDS organizations . . . have lost enormous amounts of funding to marriage equality.

Yasmin: It is probably true that hate crimes legislation and anti-bullying laws in Washington are connected to gay marriage—but that is exactly the problem. Marriage solidifies the idea that the "inclusion" of LGBT people is the solution, and it has been accompanied by a push for inclusion in the military and in hate crimes and anti-bullying legislation. But this ignores the fundamental inequality perpetuated by these institutions—marriage, the military, the criminal justice system.

Hate crimes and anti-bullying legislation are punitive measures that will drive the prison-industrial complex and the school-to-prison pipeline.

So how did the push for inclusion in these institutions become so central to today's LGBT movement?

Kenyon: The queer movement was once very much a part of the Left. But as the AIDS epidemic began to impact gay men irrespective of economic or social class, it drew a lot of conservative, wealthy, white gays into the movement, and there was a real debate amongst radical and more conservative segments. As a result, we saw the movement gravitate toward issues involving white folks' understanding of citizenship: marriage, military service and, to some extent, hate-crime legislation. This is not to say that people of color haven't fought for those things, but certainly not as ends in and of themselves. AIDS organizations, meanwhile, have lost enormous amounts of funding to marriage equality.

Josh: I don't think the emergence of the marriage equality movement has been the outgrowth of political analysis as much as it has been driven by the passion of human couples wishing to marry. There is, fundamentally, a stigma in not having the ability to choose or not choose marriage.

Yasmin: But the gay marriage movement can't have it both ways, arguing on one hand that there is this tremendous stigma, but on the other hand that people can just choose whether or not to marry. The gay marriage movement wants to pretend that marriage has somehow changed, but it also is invoking this very 1950s narrative that unmarried people are unworthy of respect.

How do you see this split over the marriage issue impacting the future direction of LGBT organizing?

Kenyon: The marriage equality movement has increased the identification of white gays and lesbians as members of the suburban middle class and, particularly in urban environments, we're seeing growing conflict over gentrification and other issues with black and brown LGBT youth.

Josh: But especially for LGBT people who are white or middle class, the battle for marriage equality has opened their eyes to other forms of oppression. Those of us who work on marriage equality must remind everyone that this is not the ultimate goal of the LGBT movement. But it is an essential ingredient—we need to build political power, not destroy it with a circular firing squad. And we absolutely need to talk about healthcare, but I think we do a disservice when we suggest marriage equality is only about healthcare.

Yasmin: It is worth remembering, though, that the AIDS movement once argued for universal healthcare, and that argument has now dropped out of the picture. Looking into the future, I see gay marriage furthering the neoliberal state. The great irony is, I may see marriage equality in the next 20 years in the United States, but I will likely never see universal healthcare in my lifetime.

Same-Sex Marriage Is Good for the Economy

Bryce Covert

Bryce Covert is the economic policy editor for Think Progress, *a political blog from the Center for American Progress, a progressive public policy research and advocacy organization.*

On Wednesday [June 26, 2013], the Supreme Court ruled that the Defense of Marriage Act [DOMA], a federal law defining marriage as between a man and a woman, is unconstitutional while also dismissing the Proposition 8 case, effectively making it legal again for gay couples to get married in California.

These historic decisions mean so much to America's gay and lesbian couples. But they will also mean something for the federal budget and the economy at large. Without DOMA, the federal government will now give gay couples who are legally married in their home states benefits they had previously been denied. Those getting married in California will have an impact too.

In 2004, the Congressional Budget Office (CBO) looked at what it would mean for the federal government to recognize same sex marriages. In all, this would impact 1,138 statutory provisions in which marriage is a factor in determining benefits, including perhaps most prominently Social Security and federal taxes. The CBO found a slightly positive impact on the budget if same-sex marriages were to be legalized in all states and recognized by the federal government: an extra $1 billion each year for the next ten years. It estimates that the government would see a small increase in tax revenues: $500 million to $700 million annually from 2011 to 2014 depending on the fate of the [former president George W.] Bush tax cuts (which were law at the time of the report).

Net Savings Expected

The government would have to spend more on Social Security and the Federal Employees Health Benefits program, but it would also save money when it came to safety net programs such as Supplemental Security Income, Medicaid, and Medicare. On net, gay marriage would reduce spending by about $100 million to $200 million a year from 2010 to 2014.

The savings in programs that help low-income families come from the fact that gay and lesbian couples are more likely to live in poverty. As Matt Yglesias has written at *Slate*, a study from the Williams Institute at UCLA found that 7.6 percent of lesbian couples live in poverty, compared to 5.7 percent of married opposite-sex couples. It also found that nearly a quarter of children living with a male same-sex couple and just under 20 percent of those living with a female same-sex couple live in poverty, compared to just 12.1 percent of children living with married heterosexual couples. This means they're more likely to rely on government benefits: 2.2 percent of women in lesbian couples receive cash assistance, versus 0.8 percent of women in opposite-sex couples, with a similar difference for men. Marriage reduces the likelihood that couples live in poverty and comes with important financial benefits.

All signs point to a positive economic impact from allowing gay men and lesbians to marry the people they love.

States Would Also Benefit

States would also see a substantial benefit. A 2009 report on marriage equality in Maine found that allowing same-sex couples to marry would increase the state budget by $7.9 million a year, a substantial sum on the state level. This comes not just from an increase in income tax revenue when couples file jointly—$69,110 per year—but also an estimated $60 million spent on weddings and tourism over three years, which could generate $3.1 million in sales tax revenue, and $538,193 in marriage license fees over three years.

In fact, a year after New York passed the Marriage Equality Act, gay marriages generated $259 million in economic impact in New York City alone.

On the business side, a report from the Human Rights Campaign found that while employers will likely have to pay more for benefits, they will have a negligible impact on costs. "In fact, because same-sex couples make up such a small percentage of the U.S. population," it notes, "the business benefits costs of allowing same-sex couples to marry will be no greater than the costs caused by fluctuations in the U.S. heterosexual marriage rates."

The Supreme Court decisions in no way guaranteed the ability for same-sex couples to get married in all 50 states, so many of the economic benefits are yet to be realized. But with DOMA struck down and 13 states legally allowing gay marriage [at the time of this writing], including California after the Proposition 8 ruling, the impacts are still likely to be felt in government coffers at both the federal and state level. All signs point to a positive economic impact from allowing gay men and lesbians to marry the people they love.

Same-Sex Marriage Does Not Help the Economy

National Organization for Marriage

The National Organization for Marriage is a national nonprofit that strongly opposes same-sex marriage and is fighting for a formal definition of marriage as the union of one man and one woman.

Is enacting same-sex marriage laws a good strategy for revitalizing a state's economy?

Some have proposed it would be, including the governor of Rhode Island, activist groups and even some business leaders. In New York, twenty-five business leaders wrote an open letter to urge the legislature to enact a same-sex marriage law. Their letter said, "In an age where talent determines the economic winners, great states and cities must demonstrate a commitment to creating an open, healthy and equitable environment in which to live and work. As other states, cities and countries across the world extend marriage rights regardless of sexual orientation, it will become increasingly difficult to recruit the best talent if New York cannot offer the same benefits and protection." In Indiana, executives of Cummins Inc. and Eli Lilly Co. offered testimony before the Senate Judiciary Committee arguing that a proposed amendment defining marriage as the union of a man and a woman would hurt businesses in the state by tarnishing Indiana's reputation.

The link between redefining marriage and creating an environment favorable to job and business growth is not intuitive but these voices are so insistent, it has begun to develop into a recurring theme.

National Organization for Marriage, "Is Gay Marriage Good for the Economy?" Research Brief, Vol. 2. No. 1, NationForMarriage.org, March 2012. Copyright © 2012 by the National Organization for Marriage. All rights reserved. Reproduced by permission.

This policy brief will examine evidence of business environment in states with same-sex marriage and states without (particularly those with marriage amendments which prevent the recognition of gay marriage) to determine whether a pattern of increased economic vitality is associated with redefining marriage.

Of the ten indicators of a positive business environment we examine here, states with marriage amendments are overrepresented on the positive lists of six and proportionately represented on the other four.

Ten Economic Indicators

For indicators of a state's business environment, we have looked at ten factors:

- CEO rankings of the states
- State GDP
- Unemployment rates
- Domestic migration
- Rates of public employment
- State and local tax burden
- Economic development rankings
- Middle-class job growth
- Overall job growth
- Per capita income growth

These indicators make abundantly clear that states with same-sex marriage are in no better position than states with marriage amendments or which do not recognize same-sex marriage. In fact, on a number of indicators, states with same-sex marriage are in worse shape.

This does not, of course, establish causation. The point of this brief is not to do so but rather to examine claims of causation made by others who claim that redefining marriage will help a state's economy.

We found that on six measures (CEO grading, domestic migration, public employment, middle-class job growth, overall job growth, and income growth), none of the six states with gay marriage appeared in the list of top states. States with gay marriage make up twelve percent of the total states but make up thirty percent of the bottom states in four indicators (CEO grading, domestic migration, public employment and tax burden) of the five which included low rankings. One state with same-sex marriage (New Hampshire) is counted among the states with the lowest tax burden. On a more positive note, states with same-sex marriage are disproportionately represented in the top states in GDP growth and on the list of enterprising states (twenty percent). Same-sex marriage states make up thirty percent of the states with the best rates of unemployment. . . .

States Without Same-Sex Marriage Fare Better

States with marriage amendments make up sixty percent of the total number of states. They make up ninety percent of the top states in overall job growth, eighty percent of the top states in four categories (CEO grading, domestic migration, public employment, and personal income growth), seventy percent in middle-class job growth, and are proportionately represented in four categories (GDP growth, low unemployment, tax burden, enterprising states). Marriage amendment states are not underrepresented in the positive side of any category. These states make up disproportionately low percentages of the states in the bottom rankings for tax burden (twenty percent), CEO rankings (forty percent), public employment (fifty percent) and domestic migration (fifty percent). These states are overrepresented among the states with highest unemployment (eighty percent).

In summary, of the ten indicators of a positive business environment we examine here, states with marriage amendments are overrepresented on the positive lists of six and proportionately represented on the other four. They are overrepresented on one of the five indicators with a bottom states list.

On the indicators, states with same-sex marriage are overrepresented on the positive lists of three, and underrepresented on the top lists of seven (with only one of these seven including a same-sex marriage state). Same-sex marriage states are overrepresented on the bottom lists of four of the five states with a low ranking category and roughly proportionately represented on the other bottom list.

These statistics make clear that there is no correlation between states with same-sex marriage and positive indicators for business climate.

Marriage Equality Is Important for Transgender People

Matt Wood

Matt Wood is a staff attorney at the Transgender Law Center, where his work focuses on health and employment law.

Marriage for same-sex couples can be a divisive issue—not just for straight people, but among LGBT communities as well. While many LGBT people were thrilled when Maryland and Washington joined the growing list of states affirming marriage equality, others continue to question the logic of spending so much time and money on the marriage effort when other issues, like health care access and economic inequality, are more pressing for many of us.

This issue can seem particularly remote from the daily concerns of many members of transgender communities. A recent survey on transgender discrimination conducted by the National Center for Transgender Equality and the National Gay and Lesbian Task Force revealed that transgender people are likely to live in extreme poverty, to be under- or unemployed, to be denied health care and housing, and to be harassed in school. Chillingly, a staggering 41% of survey respondents reported attempting suicide. (The full report is available online at http://www.thetaskforce.org.)

It's no wonder that some transgender people are frustrated by the significant resources that primarily lesbian and gay organizations have devoted to marriage equality efforts in recent years, a concern also raised by LGBT people of color, youth, and people living with HIV/AIDS. In the shadow of pervasive poverty and despair, and with virtually no national conversation about transgender rights, transgender community members see the allocation of scarce LGBT movement resources (staff time, community money, political will) on marriage as misplaced at best.

Many Transgender Couples Are Legally Same-Sex

While this frustration is understandable, it may be short-sighted. First, it ignores the fact that many transgender people are also lesbian, gay, or bisexual, or in relationships that the government views as legally "same-sex," even if the partners consider themselves to be different sex.

For instance, a marriage between a trans man and a non-trans woman might or might not be legally recognized as a valid different-sex marriage. That's because the standard for having a person's gender identity legally recognized depends upon where they were born, and where they currently live. While most states permit a person to change the gender on their birth certificate, many require the person to have some kind of medical intervention in order to do so—medical intervention that many transgender people may not be able to afford, or may not want. Some states, including Idaho, Tennessee, and Ohio, refuse to change the gender marker on birth certificates.

When laws that limit access to marriage based on gender are repealed, transgender people benefit.

When one spouse is transgender and the other is not, a marriage between two people with the same gender identity may also be considered legally same-sex or different-sex depending on whether the transgender spouse transitioned before or after the marriage. For example, a marriage that was considered a valid different-sex marriage when the spouses got married might get challenged as an invalid same-sex marriage after one spouse transitions.

It's a longstanding principle of family law that a marriage that was valid when entered remains valid forever, and can only end through death, divorce, or annulment. Yet we at Transgender Law Center regularly hear from people whose marriages have been improperly reclassified as "domestic partnerships" by their employer because of one spouse's gender change, and who have then been denied health benefits from the employer, or who are denied spousal Social Security benefits after one spouse transitions.

Ultimately, whether a transgender person's marriage will be recognized as valid or not often depends on what state they live in, what medical procedures they've undergone, and whether or not an employer or insurer or family member chooses to challenge their marriage's validity.

Marriage Equality Would Help

None of this would matter, though, if marriage between same-sex couples were recognized by all states and by the federal government. When laws that limit access to marriage based on gender are repealed, transgender people benefit. And as long as marriage remains the primary means for the state to distribute health, retirement, education, and other social benefits—despite the fact that this means of distributing important benefits may be fundamentally unfair—transgender people should have equal access to those benefits and resources, regardless of each partner's legal gender.

Of course, marriage equality won't solve everything for transgender people. Having access to health care through a spouse's insurance—for those people who happen to be married and happen to have a spouse whose employer provides health insurance—will not guarantee coverage for transition-related care. It won't ensure culturally-competent health care providers for transgender patients. Marriage equality won't end bullying in schools, and it won't automatically create jobs in a shrinking economy or, for that matter, create transgender antidiscrimination laws in the 34 states that don't have them. But marriage equality will, by definition, lessen government scrutiny into what a person's legal gender is. And ultimately, any decrease in the government's regulation of gender is good for all LGBT people.

Organizations to Contact

The editors have compiled the following list of organizations concerned with the issues debated in this book. The descriptions are derived from materials provided by the organizations. All have publications or information available for interested readers. The list was compiled on the date of publication of the present volume; names, addresses, phone and fax numbers, and e-mail and Internet addresses may change. Be aware that many organizations take several weeks or longer to respond to inquiries, so allow as much time as possible.

American Civil Liberties Union (ACLU)—LGBT Project
125 Broad St., 18th Floor, New York, NY   10004
(212) 549-2500
e-mail: info@aclu.org
website: www.aclu.org/lgbt-rights

Through activism in courts, legislatures, and communities nationwide, the American Civil Liberties Union (ACLU) works to defend and preserve the individual rights and liberties that the Constitution and laws of the United States guarantee to everyone. The ACLU website has an extensive collection of reports, briefings, and news updates related to gay rights and marriage equality. Content specifically related to same-sex marriage includes the publications "If You Think Marriage Doesn't Matter—Think Again" and "DOMA Zombies Surface in Congress." The LGBT Project is a special campaign of the ACLU dedicated to the establishment of a society in which all people—regardless of sexual orientation or gender identity—have full constitutional rights of equality, privacy and personal autonomy, and freedom of expression and association.

Cato Institute
1000 Massachusetts Ave. NW, Washington, DC   20001-5403
(202) 842-0200 • fax: (202) 842-3490
website: www.cato.org

The Cato Institute is a libertarian public policy research foundation dedicated to limiting the role of government, protecting individual liberties, and promoting free markets. The Institute commissions a variety of publications, including books, monographs, briefing papers, and other studies. Among its publications are the quarterly magazine *Regulation*, the bimonthly *Cato Policy Report*, and the periodic *Cato Journal*. It offers an extensive selection of materials online, including dozens related to same-sex marriage. Recent commentary pieces include "Once-Loud Opposition to Gay Marriage Has Quieted" and "Republicans, Gay Marriage and the Sound of Social Change."

Family Research Council (FRC)
801 G St. NW, Washington, DC   20001
(202) 393-2100 • fax: (202) 393-2134
website: www.frc.org

Founded in 1983, the Family Research Council (FRC) is a nonprofit organization that is dedicated to advancing faith, family, and freedom in both public policy and culture from a Christian worldview. FRC is one of the country's leading groups opposing same-sex marriage and the organization's website features more than seven hundred research papers, essays, news updates, and blog posts related to the topic.

Focus on the Family
8605 Explorer Dr., Colorado Springs, CO   80920-1051
(800) 232-6459 • fax: (719) 531-3424
website: www.focusonthefamily.com

Focus on the Family is a conservative Christian organization that promotes traditional family values including heterosexual marriage. It is a source of a wide range of information delineating arguments against the legalization of same-sex marriage. Related publications available on the organization's website include "The Marriage Debate: Answers to Your Questions," "Collateral Damage? Children with a Gay Parent Speak Out," and "My Spouse Struggles with Homosexuality."

Freedom to Marry

155 West 19th St., 2nd Floor, New York, NY   10011
(212) 851-8418 • fax: (646) 375-2069
website: www.freedomtomarry.org

Founded in 2003 by Evan Wolfson, an attorney and gay-rights activist whom many consider to be the father of the same-sex marriage movement, Freedom to Marry is a nonprofit that campaigns for the right of same-sex couples to marry in states nationwide. The organization's website features information about its activities and programs as well as an extensive collection of FAQs, policy and legal updates, fact sheets, studies, blogs, and resources related to the campaign for marriage equality.

Gay and Lesbian Advocates and Defenders (GLAD)

30 Winter St., Suite 800, Boston, MA   02108
(617) 426-1350 • fax: (617) 426-3594
e-mail: gladlaw@glad.org
website: www.glad.org

Founded in 1978, Gay and Lesbian Advocates and Defenders (GLAD) is a nonprofit legal rights organization that works to end discrimination based on sexual orientation, HIV status, and gender identity and expression. GLAD was instrumental in winning marriage rights for same-sex couples in Massachusetts and was involved in successful legal challenges to the Defense of Marriage Act (DOMA). The organization's website features an archive of documents related to its activities as well as a collection of fact sheets, webinars, and other materials explaining the legal benefits, protections, rights, and rules that affect married same-sex couples since DOMA was struck down.

The Heritage Foundation

214 Massachusetts Ave. NE, Washington, DC   20002-4999
(202) 546-4400
e-mail: info@heritage.org
website: www.heritage.org

The Heritage Foundation is a conservative think tank that develops—and advocates for—public policies that promote the ideals of free enterprise, limited government, individual freedom, traditional American values, and a strong national defense. The organization strongly opposes same-sex marriage and its website includes hundreds of issue briefs, research papers, commentaries, blog posts, and infographics related to the topic.

Human Rights Campaign (HRC)
1640 Rhode Island Ave. NW, Washington, DC   20036-3278
(800) 777-4723
website: www.hrc.org

Founded in 1980, Human Rights Campaign (HRC) is the country's largest organization devoted to achieving full civil rights for lesbian, gay, bisexual, and transgender Americans. The organization engages in political advocacy and grassroots campaigns with more than 1.5 million members and supporters nationwide. HRC has been heavily involved in various legal battles related to marriage equality and other issues concerning gay rights. A special section of the group's website is devoted to same-sex marriage and includes news and legislative updates, position statements, and an interactive map that allows site visitors to learn about the status of same-sex marriage in each state.

National Organization for Marriage (NOM)
2029 K St. NW, Suite 300, Washington, DC   20006
(888) 894-3604 • fax: (888) 894-3604
e-mail: contact@nationformarriage.org
website: www.nationformarriage.org

The National Organization for Marriage (NOM) was launched in 2007 in response to what the founders called "the growing need for an organized opposition to same-sex marriage in state legislatures." NOM provides educational materials, political messaging assistance, and other resources to defeat same-sex marriage initiatives at the federal, state, and local levels.

The organization's website features daily news updates and calls to action, a frequently updated blog and Twitter feed, and a wide variety of research briefs, talking points, and other materials related to the defense of traditional marriage.

Pew Research Center (PRC)
1615 L St. NW, Suite 700, Washington, DC   20036
(202) 419-4300 • fax: (202) 419-4349
website: www.pewresearch.org

Pew Research Center (PRC) is a nonpartisan research organization that informs the public about the issues, attitudes, and trends shaping America and the world. It conducts public opinion polling, demographic research, media content analysis, and other empirical social science research. Pew Research does not take policy positions; it is a subsidiary of the Pew Charitable Trusts, an independent nonprofit research organization. PRC has examined and reported on various aspects of the effort to legalize same-sex marriage both in the United States and elsewhere and its website features more than a thousand publications related to the topic, including a wide variety of fact sheets, reports, and studies.

Bibliography

Books

M.V. Lee Badgett   *When Gay People Get Married: What Happens When Societies Legalize Same-Sex Marriage*. New York: New York University Press, 2009.

Jo Becker   *Forcing the Spring: Inside the Fight for Marriage Equality*. New York: Penguin, 2014.

Mary Bernstein and Verta Taylor   *The Marrying Kind?: Debating Same-Sex Marriage Within the Lesbian and Gay Movement*. Minneapolis: University of Minnesota Press, 2013.

David Blankenhorn   *The Future of Marriage*. New York: Encounter Books, 2010.

Margot Canaday   *The Straight State: Sexuality and Citizenship in Twentieth-Century America*. Princeton, NJ: Princeton University Press, 2011.

George Chauncey   *Why Marriage: The History Shaping Today's Debate over Gay Equality*. New York: Basic Books, 2009.

Ryan Conrad, ed.   *Against Equality: Queer Critiques of Gay Marriage*. Lewiston, ME: Against Equality Publishing Collective, 2010.

Joel Derfner | *Lawfully Wedded Husband: How My Gay Marriage Will Save the American Family.* Madison: University of Wisconsin Press, 2013.

Sherif Girgis, Ryan T. Anderson, and Robert P. George | *What Is Marriage? Man and Woman: A Defense.* New York: Encounter Books, 2012.

Michael J. Klarman | *From the Closet to the Altar: Courts, Backlash, and the Struggle for Same-Sex Marriage.* New York: Oxford University Press, 2012.

Jason Pierceson | *Same-Sex Marriage in the United States: The Road to the Supreme Court and Beyond.* Lanham, MD: Rowman & Littlefield, 2014.

Daniel W. Rivers | *Radical Relations: Lesbian Mothers, Gay Fathers, and Their Children in the United States Since World War II.* Chapel Hill: University of North Carolina Press, 2013.

Rodger Streitmatter | *Outlaw Marriages: The Hidden Histories of Fifteen Extraordinary Same-Sex Couples.* Boston: Beacon, 2013.

Periodicals and Internet Sources

Halimah Abdullah | "The President and the Nation Have Evolved on Same-Sex Marriage," CNN, March 1, 2013. www.cnn.com.

Alex Altman and   "In Landmark Ruling, Supreme
Zeke Miller   Court Strikes Down Defense of
                   Marriage Act," *Time*, June 26, 2013.

Brandon   "Being Against Gay Marriage Doesn't
Ambrosino   Make You a Homophobe," *Atlantic*,
                   December 13, 2013.

Arguing Equality   "An Interactive Web Guide to
                   Understanding and Presenting the
                   Case for Same-Sex Marriage," 2014.
                   www.arguingequality.org.

Ronald Bailey   "The Science on Same-Sex Marriage,"
                   Wall Street Journal, April 3, 2013.

Aaron Blake   "Georgia GOP Chair: Straight People
                   Could Abuse Gay Marriage for
                   Benefits," *Washington Post*, April 1,
                   2013.

David   "A Call for a New Conversation on
Blankenhorn   Marriage," Institute for American
et al.   Values, 2013.
                   www.americanvalues.org.

Michelle   "Methodist Pastor Found Guilty at
Boorstein   Church Trial for Officiating at Gay
                   Son's Wedding," *Washington Post*,
                   November 18, 2013.

Michelle   "Same-Sex Marriage Again an Issue
Boorstein   for Religious Charities," *Washington
                   Post*, July 12, 2011.

Dean Burnett   "How Same-Sex Marriage Causes
                   Floods," *Guardian*, January 21, 2014.

Jackie Calmes and Peter Baker	"Obama Says Same-Sex Marriage Should Be Legal," *New York Times*, May 9, 2012.
George Chauncey	"The Long Road to Marriage Equality," *New York Times*, June 26, 2013.
Philip N. Cohen	"Same-Sex Marriage and Children, What We Don't Know Shouldn't Hurt Us," *Huffington Post*, May 11, 2009. www.huffingtonpost.com.
Nicholas Confessore	"Business Leaders, in Letter, Will Urge Albany to Legalize Gay Marriage," *New York Times*, April 28, 2011.
Charlie Cook	"My Evolution on Gay Rights," *National Journal*, January 23, 2014.
David Crary and Holbrook Mohr	"Next Step for Same-Sex Marriage: The Right to Divorce," *Denver Post*, December 1, 2013.
Drew DeSilver	"A Global Snapshot of Same-Sex Marriage," Pew Research Center, June 4, 2013. www.pewresearch.org.
Ariane DeVogue	"Obama's Evolution on Gay Marriage," ABC News, May 13, 2013. http://abcnews.go.com.
Lance Dickie	"Same-Sex Couples Strengthen and Affirm Basic Family Values," *Seattle Times*, January 19, 2012.

Steve Dinnen	"Gay Marriage 'Tourism': How Big an Economic Boom for States?," *Christian Science Monitor*, September 24, 2013.
Bryan Fischer	"Why Same-Sex Marriage Is Bad for Children," Renew America, July 7, 2008. www.renewamerica.com.
Jon Gillooly	"Cobb Sounds Off as Facebook Goes Red in Support of Gay Marriage," *Marietta Daily Journal*, April 1, 2013.
GLAAD	"Frequently Asked Questions: Defense of Marriage Act (DOMA)," 2013. www.glaad.org.
Eliza Gray	"Edith Windsor, the Unlikely Activist," *Time*, December 11, 2013.
Jesse Green	"From 'I Do' to 'I'm Done,'" *New York Magazine*, February 24, 2013.
Sally Hansell	"Facebook War: Blue Crosses Fight Red Equal Signs," *Huffington Post*, April 3, 2013. www.huffingtonpost.com.
Jeff Jacoby	"The Slippery Slope of Gay Marriage Has Begun," *Boston Globe*, December 22, 2013.
Jeffrey M. Jones	"Same-Sex Marriage Support Solidifies Above 50% in U.S.," Gallup, May 13, 2013. www.gallup.com.
Jillian Keenan	"Legalize Polygamy! No. I Am Not Kidding," *Slate*, April 15 2013. www.slate.com.

Paul Kengor   "Liberals Embrace Same-Sex Marriage and Its Consequences for Families," *Blaze*, June 27, 2013. www.theblaze.com.

Ed Kilgore   "The Hypocrisy of 'States' Rights' Conservatives: The 10th Amendment Is Sacred to the Right—Except When It Comes to Fighting Abortion and Gay Rights," *Salon*, August 7, 2011. www.salon.com.

Chris Kirk and Hanna Rosin   "Does Gay Marriage Destroy Marriage?," *Slate*, May 23, 2012. www.slate.com.

John Klar   "Proving Gay Marriage Wrong," Charisma News, January 6, 2014. www.charismanews.com.

Peter LaBarbera   "'Gay Marriage' and Distant Consequences: Homosexuality, Sexual Immorality and the Downfall of American Civilization," Americans for Truth, August 9, 2013. http://americansfortruth.com.

Michael A. Lindenberger   "In Court Victories for Gay Marriage, Signs of the Longer War to Come," *Time*, June 27, 2013.

Michal A. Lindenberger   "Why California's Gay-Marriage Ban Was Upended," *Time*, August 5, 2010.

Murray Lipp   "Same-Sex Marriage Helps Keep Binational Couples Together," *Huffington Post*, June 24, 2013. www.huffingtonpost.com.

Kathryn Jean Lopez	"The Politics of the New Normal: Maggie Gallagher on Marriage," *National Review*, March 26, 2013.
Tom McFeely	"Needed: A Federal Marriage Amendment," *National Catholic Register*, April 17, 2009.
Tony Merevick	"They Told Us Marriage Equality Is Not an African-American Issue," *Chicago Phoenix*, March 20, 2013.
Jim Morrill	"NC Gay Married Couples Face Multiple Tax Returns," *Charlotte Observer*, December 29, 2013.
William Murchison	"The Gay Marriage Sham," *Patriot Post*, July 2, 2013.
Brian Mustanski	"New Study Suggests Bans on Gay Marriage Hurt Mental Health of LGB People," *Psychology Today*, March 22, 2010.
Frank Newport	"For First Time, Majority of Americans Favor Legal Gay Marriage," Gallup, May 20, 2011. www.gallup.com.
Nolo Press	"Same-Sex Marriage: Developments in the Law," 2014. www.nolo.com.
Brendan O'Neill	"It Is Moronic to Compare Opposition to Gay Marriage with Opposition to Interracial Marriage," *Telegraph*, February 16, 2012.

Kathleen Parker	"Same-Sex Marriage Can Help Save the Institution," *Washington Post*, January 29, 2013.
Sarah Parnass	"Republicans Predict Fraud, Bestiality If Gay Marriage Is Legalized," ABC News, April 4, 2013. http://abcnews.go.com.
Eyder Peralta	"Holder Says Federal Government Will Recognize Michigan Gay Marriages," National Public Radio, March 28, 2014. www.npr.org.
David Pettinicchio	"An Anti-Gay Marriage Movement?," *Mobilizing Ideas*, June 30, 2013. http://mobilizingideas.wordpress.com.
ProCon.org	"Gay Marriage Timeline: History of the Same-Sex Marriage Debate," September 18, 2013. www.gaymarriage.procon.org.
Mark Regnerus	"Queers as Folk: Does It Really Make No Difference If Your Parents Are Straight or Gay?," *Slate*, June 11, 2012. www.slate.com.
Reuters	"Timeline of Gay Marriage in the United States," June 26, 2013. www.reuters.com.
Nicholas Riccardi	"How a Wedding Cake Became a Cause," *San Francisco Chronicle*, April 5, 2014.
Travis Rowley	"Gay Marriage Is a Sham," Go Local, January 5, 2013. www.golocalprov .com.

William Saletan — "Back in the Gay—Does a New Study Indict Gay Parenthood or Make a Case for Gay Marriage?," *Slate*, June 11, 2012. www.slate.com.

Alex Seitz-Wald — "Evangelicals Are Winning the Gay Marriage Fight—in Africa and Russia," *National Journal*, January 23, 2014.

Ari Shapiro — "Gay Marriage and the Evolving Language of Love," National Public Radio, March 29, 2013. www.npr.org.

Ilya Shapiro — "Pro-Marriage-Equality, Pro-Religious Liberty," Cato Institute, August 1, 2013. www.cato.org.

Philip Shishkin — "The Battle over Benefits for Same-Sex Spouses," *Wall Street Journal*, May 21, 2009.

Steve Snyder — "Lebanon County Pastor Frank Schaefer Receives Suspension," *Lebanon Daily News*, November 20, 2013.

Erin Solaro — "Marriage Is a Human Right, Not a Religious Issue," *Seattle Post Intelligencer*, December 12, 2008.

Marc D. Stern — "Will Gay Rights Infringe on Religious Liberty?," CNN, March 25, 2013. www.cnn.com.

Mark Joseph Stern — "Yes, Opposing Gay Marriage Makes You a Homophobe," *Slate*, December 16, 2013. www.slate.com.

Andrew Sullivan "Why Gay Marriage Is Good for America," *Newsweek*, July 18, 2011.

Jeffrey Toobin "Adieu, DOMA!," *New Yorker*, July 8, 2013.

David Von Drehle "How Gay Marriage Won," *Time*, March 28, 2013.

Rachel Weiner "Why 'Evolution' Is a Win for Gay Marriage," *Washington Post*, April 2, 2013. www.washingtonpost.com /blogs/the-fix.

Seth Freed Wessler "DOMA Ruling Clears Path for Binational Couples," *Colorlines*, June 26, 2013. www.colorlines.com.

Pete Williams "Supreme Court's DOMA Ruling Spurs State Marriage Battle," NBC News, August 7, 2013. http:// usnews.nbcnews.com.

Edith Windsor "My Late Wife's Spirit Was with Us in Court," CNN, March 28, 2013. www.cnn.com.

Chrisopher Wolfe "What Marriage Has Become," *Public Discourse*, March 21, 2011. www .thepublicdiscourse.com.

Eric Zorn "What to Expect Now That We're Expecting Gay Marriage," *Chicago Tribune*, November 20, 2013.

Index

Equal Protection Clause of the Hawaii Constitution, 36
Equal Rights Washington, 220
Eskridge, William N., 127
Evangelical Free Church of Canada, 213
Evangelical Lutheran Church in Denmark, 83
Exclusivity marriage, 142–143

F

Family Inequality (blog), 184
Family Research Council, 24, 125
Family stability in same-sex marriage, 94–95
Farrow, Kenyon, 220–225
Federal Employees Health Benefits Program, 112, 227
Federal Marriage Amendment, 25
Federal worker benefits, 168–169
Feldblum, Chai, 147
Fenty, Adrian, 42
Focus on the Family, 24
Foster, Jodie, 52
Foster care agencies, 202–203, 209–210
Foster parents, 211–212
France, 81
Franke-Ruta, Garance, 50–60
Freedom of religion, 96
Freedom to Marry group, 17–18, 36–49
Friedes, Josh, 220–225

G

Gabbatt, Adam, 61–65
Gallagher, Maggie, 104, 109, 116–117, 119
Gallup poll, 34, 134

Garcia, Orlando, 49
Gay, Lesbian, Bisexual and Transgender News Network, 18
Gay & Lesbian Advocates & Defenders, 40
Gendered social control, 154
Gender identity, 178
Gender JUST, 220
George, Robert P., 194–197
Georgetown University, 147
Gilfoyle, Natalie F.P., 175–181
Gill v. Office of Personnel Management (2010), 42
Gingrey, Phil, 182–183
Gingrich, Newt, 25, 51, 59
Girgis, Sherif, 194–197
Glee (TV show), 19
Global recognition of same-sex marriage, 79–88
Golinski v. Office of Personnel Management (2012), 44
Goodridge v. Department of Public Health (2003), 22, 38, 203
Government Accounting Office, 27
Graff, E.J., 139
Green, Aake, 216
Gregoire, Christine, 40, 43
Grey's Anatomy (TV show), 19
Guardian (newspaper), 61, 65
Gustav-Wrathall, John, 99–102

H

Hagel, Chuck, 51, 54
Hands On Originals, 217
Hate crimes, 52–53, 132
Heitkamp, Heidi, 58
Helms, Jesse, 50
Henry, Fred, 212
Heritage Foundation, 145
Herman, Jody L., 199